The Cultural World of the Apostles

The Cultural World of the Apostles

The Second Reading, Sunday by Sunday
Year C

John J. Pilch

LITURGICAL PRESS
Collegeville, Minnesota

www.litpress.org

Cover design by David Manahan, O.S.B. Photo courtesy of Jeffrey Hutson, O.S.B.

Year A: 0-8146-2726-9
Year B: 0-8146-2781-1
Year C: 0-8146-2782-X

2	3	4	5	6	7	8	9

Library of Congress Cataloging-in-Publication Data

Pilch, John J.
    The cultural world of the apostles: the second reading,
  Sunday by Sunday, year A / John J. Pilch.
        p. cm.
    Includes bibliographical references.
    ISBN 0-8146-2726-9 (alk. paper)
    1. Bible. N.T. Epistles–Liturgical use. 2. Bible. N.T.
  Revelation–Liturgical use. 3. Bible. N.T. Epistles–History of
  contemporary events. 4. Bible. N.T. Revelation–History of
  contemporary events. 5. Middle East–Civilization–To 622. I. Title.

  BS2635.55 .P55 2001
  227'.067–dc21

                                                      00-052042

For Mary Ruzicka Crook, M.M.
masterful voice teacher
Slavic soul-mate
dear friend
and all my fellow singers and friends
in her studio,
the Baltimore Symphony Chorus,
the Baltimore Opera Company,
and every chorus with which I have sung.

"I will sing to the Lord *as long as I live" (Ps 104:33)*
with grateful appreciation for all of you.

Contents

Introduction

During a recent extended visit–my third–to Poland, I realized that I was suffering culture shock. The discovery surprised me. I was born in America of first-generation American parents, but my first language was Polish. I am fluent in that language. My formal education included fourteen years of the study of the Polish language, history, culture, and literature. In Poland, people often ask, "When did you return to Poland?" or "How long have you lived in America." They are surprised to learn that I was born in America.

As I reflected upon and analyzed my shocking experiences, it became clear to me that the pain was caused because I was misunderstanding and misinterpreting my experiences. I was insufficiently aware of the melody of the spoken language that gives nuance to spoken words. I also failed to notice nonverbal cues. Gradually I realized that this is a high-context culture; that is, people assume and take many things for granted because every one is socialized to know what is expected in each interpersonal interaction. In contrast, my own low-context American culture has socialized me to expect everything to be spelled out in great detail. In brief, I realized that I do not know the Polish social system very well, for it is the social system that gives meaning to language and human experience. The Polish-American social system in which I was socialized is somewhat helpful but mostly inadequate for Poland.

This visit differed from the others in that I was the guest of a native Pole, Dr. Jadwiga M. Rakowska. She served as a guide and informant. She explained and interpreted my puzzling experiences even though she didn't witness many of them. She recommended a newly published dictionary written for foreigners. I consulted it often during our postdinner discussions to clarify for myself nuances in this highly inflected language. Moreover, the dictionary pointed out that much of my vocabulary is "literary." In modern Poland, a new and different vocabulary has developed. I came to appreciate the value of a native cultural informant or guide.

People whose cultural background is not Mediterranean or Middle- Eastern should expect the same kind of shocking experiences when they read the Bible. If reading the Bible is not a jarring experience, that could be a clue that the reader is imposing her or his culture upon the people on the pages of their English translations. Such a reading tends to make those people "just like us." Any contemporary experience with people from others cultures should make one quite aware of the fact that "they" are not "just like us."

In my three-volume series *The Cultural World of Jesus: Sunday by Sunday* (Collegeville: The Liturgical Press, 1995–97), I tried to serve my readers as a cultural informant or guide. No, I am not a native of the Mediterranean world, but my colleagues in The Context Group and I have spent a good portion of our careers studying the writings of "ancient informants." We have helped one another discover how to imagine the appropriate cultural scenario needed in order to understand and properly interpret the people and their behaviors described in the Bible.

Even as I began that project on the Gospels, I also intended to write a similar series of cultural reflections on the second or middle readings of the three-year lectionary cycle for Sundays. The middle reading was intended by the architects of the lectionary to be independent of the other two readings. The aim was to offer a semicontinuous reading from the letters attributed to Paul (and James in Cycle B, Twenty-Second to Twenty-Sixth Sundays in Ordinary Time). First Corinthians was spread over three years, Hebrews was spread over two years (Cycles B and C), while the other letters were completed within a given year. The letters of Peter and John and selections from Revelation were assigned to the Easter and Christmas seasons (see Sloyan). Though the author of Revelation is not the apostle John but rather one who described himself as a prophet writing for fellow Jesus-prophets (Rev 1:3), and Paul the apostle also casts himself in the role of a prophet (Gal 1:15; compare Jer 1:4), the title of this present book is *The Cultural World of the Apostles*. It treats the second or middle readings for all the Sundays and some of the feasts in the Liturgical Year C.

The notion of a semicontinuous reading makes good sense. Scholars agree that in order to appreciate what a sacred author wanted to communicate, it is advisable to read that author's book or letter from beginning to end at one sitting. Given the time constraints of the liturgy, and the limited number of Sundays in a year, only parts of a letter or document are read, not the entire document. However, the architects of the lectionary did not explain why they arranged these "edited" documents in the order we find in the lectionary over the three years, or even in any given year. That order is certainly not chronological. Therefore, to help the reader understand a given document within the life-setting of its author, I give a brief indication of the probable date of that letter and some indication of the circumstances in which it was written or to which it was directed.

The principle that guided the architects of the lectionary in selecting these middle readings in the Sunday Lectionary was that they be "short and readily grasped by the people." The readings are indeed short, deliberately edited for that purpose. In many instances, however, that brevity has deprived the reader or listener of sufficient context to interpret the text-segment in a responsible way. The reading is invariably torn from its integral literary form in the letter, and sometimes verses are omitted in order to combine what remains into a reading "readily grasped by the people." As many commentators have noted, this process has unwittingly created a new scripture. These high-context documents are now raised to an even higher context! I try to present, as briefly as possible, this broader literary context for each reading as needed. (See, for example, Second Sunday of Advent.)

That the architects actually believed a brief reading could be "readily grasped by the people" is astonishing. Everyone can understand the brief English sentence: "He hit it." But without the proper context, it is entirely impossible to *interpret* this sentence. Who is he? What is it? What is the meaning of "hit"? Many of the brief readings in the lectionary contain but a few verses. Read Galatians 4:4-7 assigned for January 1: the Solemnity of the Blessed Virgin Mary, the Mother of God. Without an understanding of how young boys are raised in the Ancient Middle Eastern world, the interpretation of this passage can easily be overshadowed by Western understanding of the word "Father," and its emotional overtones. To understand the very different emotional overtones a Middle Eastern boy would assign to this word, read the comment on Hebrews 12:5-7, 11-13 (Twenty-First Sunday in Ordinary Time). Once this understanding is grasped, a reader can begin to explore the cultural significance of Paul's statement in Galatians and recognize the challenge of applying it in a different cultural context.

The architects also appear to have been totally unaware of the radically different cultural settings in which the majority of contemporary readers or listeners receive these text-segments which originated in first-century Mediterranean cultural settings. That culture is the essential context for interpreting what the sacred author intended and meant. Only when the reader or listener has grasped that meaning can the reader or listener begin to make an application to his or her own cultural context. Thus, consider the selection from Galatians 1:1-2, 6-10 assigned for the Ninth Sunday in Ordinary Time. Without an understanding of the meaning of loyalty, shame, and curse in the ancient Mediterranean world, the meaning of this passage (reshaped by the architects of the lectionary!) is completely opaque for the contemporary reader. Once these key ideas are included in the interpretation, a reader can begin to explore possible adaptations of the message for readers in a very different cultural context.

Just as in my volumes on *The Cultural World of Jesus*, so too here do I use the historical critical method supplemented by insights from cultural anthropology. One understanding of history is that things were not always the way they are now. Even in antiquity, if a reader can place Paul and his letters in chronological context, it becomes easier to notice where Paul's thinking has developed or where Paul has changed his mind. Moreover, of the letters attributed to Paul in the New Testament, scholars agree that seven are indisputably authentic: 1 Thessalonians, Galatians, 1–2 Corinthians, Philemon, Romans, and Philippians. Because the authenticity of the others is disputed, they are called the Deutero-Paulines: 2 Thessalonians, Colossians, Ephesians, 1–2 Timothy, and Titus. Hebrews is not really a letter (actually, neither is Ephesians), and scholars agree that it was not written by Paul. I indicate this kind of historical information in this book at the first verses drawn from a given document of the New Testament in the lectionary. The reader is thus encouraged to consider how far removed this text-segment may be from the time of Jesus' death, from the time of the activity of his disciples, and even from the time of the reputed author. What has developed during thirty or more years? In the case of letters written by Paul's disciples in his name (e.g., 1–2 Tim, Titus), what developments have emerged?

With due respect to the architects of the lectionary, Paul cannot be "readily grasped by the people" if those people do not share his Mediterranean cultural heritage (see Malina and Neyrey). True to his own cultural heritage, Paul is a non-introspective person who thinks as he speaks. His letters record what flowed from his mouth after a fashion we might identify as stream of consciousness. Mediterranean persons often speak while they think. They do not routinely think before speaking. Hence Paul's letters often seem illogical, contradictory, and very difficult to understand. Practically all commentators admit this.

To complicate matters, in his letters (and those of other apostles) we have only half the conversation. We do not know the statements or ideas or behaviors to which he is reacting. We have only his (accurate? or biased?) report and his interpretation of what others have said or done. The experience is similar to hearing only one side of a telephone conversation. Relying upon expert Pauline scholars such as Jerome Murphy-O'Connor or Joseph Fitzmyer, I have tried to indicate where Paul or another apostle may have been quoting an opponent. This is not always evident in the text of the lectionary or the Bible.

The Mediterranean cultural information I seek to share in these reflections is not generally available in the vast majority of commentaries or homiletic aids currently on the market. The resources and scholars upon whom I have relied are listed at the end of this volume. The information provided in traditional commentaries and homiletic aids is good and presupposed by my reflections. At the same time, cultural insights may require that a reader modify that information in reaching a final interpretation of each text-segment that will respect its original cultural setting.

At the conclusion of the reflections in *The Cultural World of Jesus,* I attempted to craft a question or thought about possible relevance or challenge to the contemporary believer in his or her culture. In this volume, I have attempted the same and something more. Though the second reading was never intended by the architects of the lectionary to be related to the gospel, nearly all the preaching I have heard in all denominations that use this or a similar lectionary attempts to relate all three readings to each other (for better or for worse!). Moreover, participants in RCIA (Rite of Christian Initiation of Adults) programs who have found my previous three volumes very helpful will probably want to relate their thoughts on the second reading with the gospel. For this reason, I have attempted to suggest such a relationship where it seems possible. Readers who use this book in line with the intention of the architects of the lectionary who never intended these readings to be related to the gospel can simply ignore the final sentence or paragraph in which I do that.

My prayer is that this volume, like its predecessors and companion *(The Cultural World of Jesus; The Cultural Dictionary of the Bible),* might contribute to an ever deeper understanding of and appreciation for our Mediterranean ancestors in the faith.

Feast of Blessed John Duns Scotus   John J. Pilch
November 8, 2003   Georgetown University

First Sunday of Advent
1 Thessalonians 3:12–4:2

In wrapping up his letter to the Thessalonians, written about 50 A.D., Paul exhorts them to "conduct yourselves" (twice!) in such a way as to please God. That English phrase "conduct yourselves" is literally in Greek "walk." This is quite likely a direct translation of a Hebrew word well known to Paul and, in fact, to all early believers in Jesus. In the Israelite tradition, "halakah" refers to legal prescriptions for conducting a life pleasing to God. The word *hlk* literally means "to walk" and the concern is how to walk in such a manner as to please God. Israelites were ever concerned with it. Jesus taught a new way of walking *(halakah)* that would please God. Thus, after Jesus' death his followers called themselves (and others identified them as) followers of the Way (Greek *hodos*, path, road, way). This is the road along which they walked to please God.

And what is central to this "way" of pleasing God? That believers in Jesus should increase and abound in love for each other (the in-group) and for all (even the out-group, quite a remarkable thing in a group-centered society). Such behavior would strengthen their hearts and render them pure, holy, blameless in holiness in the sight of God the Father as they await the coming of the Lord Jesus with his holy ones. Behind these concerns lies Paul's basic understanding of sin as "leaven" (a polluting and corrupting agent) and "gangrene" (see 2 Tim 2:17, a life-threatening condition). It cannot be tolerated and must be rooted out!

1

Luke's Jesus cautions in today's gospel (Luke 21:25-28, 34-36) against allowing one's heart to become drowsy from carousing, drunkenness, and the anxieties of daily life. These are to be avoided like leaven and gangrene. The vigilance encouraged will help believers to strive to remain blameless in holiness, as Paul dictated.

Second Sunday of Advent
Philippians 1:4-6, 8-11

[Contemporary scholarship identifies three distinct letters in Philippians: Letter A = 4:10-20 (a receipt for aid, in which Paul acknowledges receiving a gift); Letter B = 1:1–3:1a; 4:4-7, 21-23 (in which Paul, having heard of problems in the community, exhorts to unity and joy); and Letter C = 3:1b–4:3, 8-9 (in which Paul addresses problems caused by wandering Judaizing missionaries). Scholars who identify three letters date A and B probably from A.D. 54–57; Letter C some time later, perhaps A.D. 57–58. All came from Paul imprisoned in Ephesus. Those who identify two letters (combining B and C into one–B), date A to A.D. 58–60 and B to A.D. 62 when Paul was imprisoned in Rome. Cycle C draws from letters B and C.]

Paul writes this letter from prison (probably in Rome) to a community that was dear to his heart and brought him much joy. These believers live in a military colony and prize their Roman citizenship. They not only accepted the gospel he preached, but shared it in turn with others and continued steadfastly in that ministry. This activity put them into a special relationship with Paul (*koinonia* is the Greek word, meaning fellowship) and expresses confidence that God will bless and continue to bring their ministry to fruition. For this Paul offers thanks to God. An expression of thanksgiving customarily follows after the introduction and greeting in most of Paul's letters.

Next Paul utters an intercessory prayer rooted in his deep affection for them. Recalling that our non-introspective Middle Eastern ancestors in the faith judged people by external criteria, Paul gives evidence that he considers the Philippians to be totally and completely wholesome. He prays that their love (deriving from the heart-eyes symbolic body zone) should increase in understanding (heart-eyes) and every kind of perception (heart-eyes) to discern what is of value (heart-eyes) and be pure (heart-eyes) and blameless (hands-feet) for the day of Christ (vv. 9-10). Their commitment to promoting the gospel (mouth-ears) continues undeterred by reversals or negative experiences (v. 5). Moreover, Paul's intense emotional sentiments expressed in the thanksgiving and prayer serve as glue to strengthen the bond that already exists between him and his beloved community.

The Baptist's preaching reported by Luke in today's gospel (3:1-6) may well have been echoed by Paul in his evangelization and by his beloved Philippians as well. The Good News needs to be disseminated. Who could do it better than those who understand and experience what it is all about?

Third Sunday of Advent
Philippians 4:4-7

The Latin version of this reading which was used on the third Sunday of Advent before the restoration of a three-year lectionary cycle gave the day its distinctive name: Gaudete Sunday. These verses served as the introit and the epistle in those years, thus they were the first words the worshiping community heard: an exhortation to rejoice! Joy permeates Paul's "letter B" to the Philippians, and in these concluding verses Paul commands them to rejoice (Latin: *gaudete*) in the Lord. The main reason for rejoicing is for all the good that the Lord has effected in this community.

Paul also exhorts them to show "kindness" to all. The Greek word translated as kindness belongs to at least two semantic domains: moral and ethical qualities, and characteristics of interpersonal behavior. Basically, the Greek word means "gracious forbearing." In English, forbearance implies restraint under provocation and refraining from retaliation for a wrong. The Philippian believers were tested by antagonism from fellow citizens (1:28-30) squabbling within the community about how to be good believers. They also experienced threats from itinerant preachers who promoted acceptance of Judaic practices that Paul taught them to reject. To be graciously forbearing as they were in all these experiences was an admirable trait that Paul hopes they will continue to extend to all.

Strength for such behavior will come from the fact that "the Lord is near." While this sentiment reflects the early

belief that the risen Jesus was to return again very soon, perhaps here it primarily reminds the Philippians that the Lord
is indeed in their midst. This is a constant presence, a source
of encouragement and support for the community at all
times. It is especially important in a community that might
be in danger of being torn apart by strong convictions of certain members who in turn might be inclined to dismiss other
members as less perfect with a faith less solid than their own.
The admirable optimism that comes from a conviction of
being right should not blind believers to the good that happens in other circles of the community. The Lord is near and
ever ready to respond to prayer and petition. The nearness
of the Lord should dispel anxiety.

In today's gospel (Luke 3:10-18), the Baptist suggests concrete behaviors that mark repentance and will prepare his
listeners for the advent of the Messiah. Paul recognized in
the Philippians a key behavior that pleases God, brings totally unimaginable peace, and keeps their hearts and minds
centered on Messiah Jesus. Come, Lord Jesus!

Fourth Sunday of Advent
Hebrews 10:5-10

[For brief introductory comments to Hebrews see Nativity: Mass during the Day.] Hebrews 8:1–10:18 is the heart of the author's explanation of the priestly deed of Jesus. It proceeds through reflection on Jeremiah 31 and interprets Jesus' death as a sacrifice that atones for sins once-and-for-always and establishes a permanent "new" covenant between God and humankind. Hebrews 10 is composed of two segments: vv. 1-4 contrast old and new to show the inadequacy of the old sacrificial cult; vv. 5-10 focus on the sacrifice of Jesus and its superiority to the old sacrifices.

The sacred author quotes loosely from Ps 40(39):7-9, and as he does throughout this letter, he interprets it to suit the message he is developing. First, he puts the verses on the lips of Jesus something like a programmatic statement of the reason for becoming incarnate. The psalmist contrasts sacrifice with his personal, voluntary obedience. The author of Hebrews replaces "ears" with "body," thus highlighting the fact that Jesus' obedience involves his total body.

The author's interpretation is distinctive. Though comparable to the pesharim (commentaries) found at Qumran, it is nevertheless different. Pesharim study the biblical text verse by verse, searching for a meaning applicable to the life of the community, to its past or present circumstances, and to its future hope. The presumption is that the ancient prophet or psalmist spoke primarily not to his time but to the future, and specifically to the Qumran community. The authors of the pesharim often read the ancient text in a way the ancient author could not have intended (at least based on the grammatical sense).

What the author of Hebrews does in his interpretation is to present two principles. First, that God did not approve all the purely external ritual principles of sacrifices required by the Law. (The psalmist did not go so far; he simply echoes traditional prophetic critiques of cult.) Second, God approves rather a ready obedience to God's will. Thus the new covenant promised by Jeremiah indicated that the old one was going to disappear (see Heb 8:13). The actual revocation of the ancient and quite ineffective way of atoning for sins to gain access to God has taken place, according to the author of Hebrews, in Jesus' obedience. By Jesus' willing obedience of God's will, he has embraced it as his very own (see Matt 26:42; John 4:34; etc.).

Today's gospel (Luke 1:39-45) reports the meeting between two women who showed themselves ready and willing to obey God's will for each. Not only is that truly honorable, as Elizabeth tells Mary, but it is also sanctifying, as the author of Hebrews notes. His creative fashioning of a programmatic statement about the purpose of the incarnation is fitting for this season. If a modern believer were asked to write such a programmatic statement about the purpose of his or her own life, how might it look?

Vigil of the Nativity
Acts 13:16-17, 22-25

Scholars agree that this "sermon" preached by Paul is in reality a Lukan composition following the pattern of earlier sermons (Acts 2:38-40; 3:19-26). Typically there are three parts: God's promise in history (vv. 16-25), the Jesus kerygma as fulfillment of the promise (vv. 26-37), and an exhortation to faith and forgiveness (vv. 38-41). Today's verses present a selective summary of history. God chose our ancestors, among whom was David, "a man after my own [God's] heart." Jesus, heralded by John, was David's descendant and savior of Israel.

What does it mean to be a person "after God's own heart"? Everything human beings know and say about God is based on human experience. In theological jargon, "all theology is analogy." Further, human experience is culturally shaped. Our non-introspective (actually, anti-introspective!) Mediterranean ancestors in the faith viewed human beings externally as composed of three interacting zones of the body: heart-eyes, mouth-ears, and hands-feet. Heart-eyes symbolized emotion-fused thought, mouth-ears self-expressive speech, and hands-feet purposeful action.

In the New Testament, God too functions in terms of these three zones. Relative to Jesus as son, the Father functions in terms of the heart-eyes zone: God "*sees* in secret" (Matt 6:18), *knows* our hearts (Luke 16:15), *loves* the world (John 3:16), *judges* each according to his deeds (1 Pet 1:17), and so on. Relative to God, Jesus as Word functions in terms of the mouth-ears zone: he reveals the Father (John 1:1ff.). The Father *has spoken* to us by a Son (Heb 1:12). In other words, Jesus is the mouth-ears of God. The hands-feet zone applied to the Father invariably refers to the Spirit who exhibits power, activity, doing, and effectiveness. The "hand [or spirit] of the Lord was upon" many of the prophets (1 Kgs 18:46; 2 Kgs 3:15; etc.). This typical Mediterranean way of viewing the human person may well be the source of the later Christian development of the notion of the Trinity.

Thus, a person "after God's own heart" is one who relates harmoniously with the divine intellect, will, judgment, conscience, personality thrust, core personality—to borrow words from Western cultural perspectives. Such a person is totally pleasing to God. The speech that Luke crafts for Paul draws this phrase from 1 Sam 13:14 where Samuel tells Saul that God has rejected him as king in favor of David. Saul tended to overstep his authority. Too often he took matters into his own hands rather than obey God's law strictly (1 Sam 13:1-15, esp. v. 14; 15:10-33). David was one who would "carry out my [God's] every wish." The gospel for this vigil (Matt 1:18-25) describes the circumstances of the birth of Jesus, one who carried out "God's every wish" even more faithfully than David. In David and Jesus modern believers face a powerful challenge to become people after God's own heart. How does that occur?

Nativity: Midnight Mass
Titus 2:11-14

[For background to the pastorals, see Twenty-Fourth Sunday in Ordinary Time.] This letter (along with 1 and 2 Timothy) has been dubbed by tradition as one of the Pastoral epistles. They have been called Pastoral epistles since the eighteenth century because they are addressed to "pastors" of early communities. For this reason, the anonymous person who wrote this letter under the name of Paul, who was already dead, is usually called "the Pastor."

The architects of the lectionary have omitted the first and very important word in today's reading: "for." In Greek this particle always points backwards. The verses that follow this word provide the motive for what preceded (vv. 1-10 are guidelines for behavior based on age and gender (older men/older women; younger men/younger women). Thus have the architects made these verses somewhat "free floating" in the liturgy.

The key word now is "appeared" (v. 11), and its tense in Greek signals a once-and-for-always perspective. How has the grace of God appeared once-and-for-always? The noun "appearance" occurs just six times in the New Testament and always in reference to Jesus. So the process by which God relates to humans (= "grace") has been revealed once and forever in Jesus, in what he said and did and means for us (= salvation).

What is God doing for us? "Training us," that is, forming us as authentic human beings in all respects: emotionally, intellectually, socially, religiously, politically, and any other way we might imagine. In modern terms, God is relating to us now holistically.

How does God train us? We must (a) reject godless ways and (b) worldly desires. Instead, on the positive side we must live (b') temperately, justly, and (a') devoutly. Notice the arrangement of ideas, so common in the Bible (a, b, b', a'). Godless ways would be equivalent to religious indifferentism or atheistic secularism. If science or some other idol usurps God's role to be in charge of life, the result is a godless way of life.

Worldly desires might be interpreted as accepting the dictates of one's culture without critical evaluation. Many people in Western culture derive a sense of self-worth from having a job or the right kind of job. Does human worth and identity depend on a job, or on something other than one's job? Instead, believers are called to lead sensible, self-controlled lives and to live justly or uprightly. This means one must live in good interpersonal relationships with other human beings. Finally, to live devoutly is to acknowledge God's reign in our personal lives. While this may sound like excessive reliance upon personal efforts, the Pastor says exactly the opposite: it is God's grace that makes good living possible. God's activity on our behalf through Jesus makes us true human beings. Moreover, God's training is effective because of Jesus' voluntary death in total obedience to the Father so that we might be cleansed and eager to do good.

This reflection on the consequences of Jesus' life and death for us is a fitting transition to the gospel (Luke 2:1-14) which announces the birth of Jesus. Clearly the feast is about much more than the joy, lights, and gifts so characteristic of the season.

Nativity: Mass at Dawn
Titus 3:4-7

Scholars recognize these verses as a popular "creed" which the Pastor inserted at this point in his letter as a comment on good deeds (3:1, 5, 8) and bad deeds (3:9). (Examples of other such creedal statements in the Pastorals would be 1 Tim 1:15; 2:4-6; 3:16; 6:12-16; 2 Tim 1:8-10; Titus 2:11-14.) Such creedal statements may have originated in the context of liturgies. If so, the Pastor's ready reliance on creeds in his instructions about proper behavior (good and bad deeds) is an excellent example of moving from liturgy to life among our ancestors in the faith.

The Pastor's creed-based observation is that good deeds by themselves don't merit anything from God (v. 5). Rather, everything is a free gift coming to us through baptism. But remember that in Mediterranean culture, there really are no free gifts. Every gift expects one in return, or at least some response. This response is "good deeds."

Once again, these verses seem well suited to the gospel (Luke 2:15-20) in which the shepherds who received word of the birth of Jesus don't just put it on their calendars or their lists of things "to do," but rather immediately (so typical of the Mediterranean culture's intense focus on the present) go to Bethlehem, see for themselves, and return glorifying and praising God. Would you consider yourself a person who acts promptly on a resolution or one who procrastinates? Would it make a difference?

Nativity: Mass during the Day
Hebrews 1:1-6

Writing in the name of Paul sometime between A.D. 60 and 100, this anonymous author has produced a masterpiece of literature and theological reflection about Jesus. These opening verses sum up the letter and the significance of today's feast: Jesus is Son and word of God, God's definitive self-disclosure. The verses are also very different in form and content from the customary opening verses of Paul's letters.

The final verses (4-6) emphasize that Jesus is superior to the angels. Indeed he is an agent of revelation far superior to the angels. (For angels as agents or mediators of revelation see 1 Kgs 13:18; Isaiah 6; Daniel 7–12; 2 Esdras 3–14.) Since the author does not engage in specific polemics, scholars have been unable to determine the reason for this emphasis upon Jesus as superior to the angels. Some scholars think this community may have been attracted to or participated in worshiping angels. The letter provides no evidence for this hypothesis. What is more likely is that the community may have thought they were worshiping with angels (e.g., Isa 6:3). This is a familiar idea in first-century Judaism which later became an element of Christian liturgical practice. Variations on the phrase "And so, with all the choirs of angels in heaven we proclaim your glory" appear in prefaces throughout the Liturgical Year. If the author thought that associating Jesus with the angels in some way minimized Jesus' role as mediator, it is surprising that he does not dwell upon it more explicitly.

The author's purpose is clear. He seeks to reinforce the sublime dimension of Jesus' exalted status which guarantees salvation to believers. This strong statement prepares the way for his subsequent presentation of Jesus' humiliation which gained that salvation for his followers.

This reading links well with the gospel (John 1:1-18), which is the classic statement of Jesus' exalted status in the New Testament. It also looks back to the gospel for the Mass at Dawn, which highlighted a special function for angels at the birth of Jesus. Given the popularity of angels in the contemporary world, Hebrews invite modern believers to examine their faith and make certain that Jesus remains central and unsurpassed as our mediator with the Father.

Sunday within the Octave of Christmas: Holy Family Sunday
1 John 3:1-2, 21-24

This is not a letter so much as it is an exhortation to Johannine believers. We do not know the author's identity; he is not the author of the gospel.

The community for which this document was intended represents a third stage of development in the Johannine community. The first phase (pre-gospel, from mid 50's to late 80's) was marked by expulsion from the synagogue (John 9:22; 16:2) and growing animosity between those who accepted Jesus as Messiah and those who didn't. Phase two is the period in which the gospel is being written (c. 90 A.D.). Scars from expulsion are slow to heal because of continuing persecution (John 16:2-3), and antipathy toward "the Judeans" on the part of believers in Jesus grows. In reaction to the rejection of Jesus, the Johannine group develops a "high Christology" (eclipsing the humanity of Jesus) which sets the group at odds with other groups that believe in Jesus. Phase three (c. 100, the time when the 3 letters of John were probably written) involves ingroup fighting between various Johannine groups who differ in their understanding and interpretation of Jesus. This is the setting for reading and appreciating 1 John.

Key to understanding these verses is a proper interpretation of the word "world" (Greek: *kosmos*). In the Hellenistic period (300 B.C. to A.D. 300), "world" referred to God's created universe, the earth on contrast to the sky, the inhabited earth,

the place of human society, and humanity. Modern understanding and usage of the word is similar. While the Johannine community sometimes used this word to refer to God's
creation (John 11:9; 17:5, 24; 21:25), most of the time it refers
to humanity, human beings. Specifically, in the Johannine
community, "world" means Israelites. "Jesus answered him
[the high priest]: 'I have spoken publicly to the world. I have
always taught in a synagogue or in the temple area where all
the Judeans gather, and in secret I have said nothing" (John
18:20). "God so loved the world [that is, the Israelites] that he
gave his only Son" (John 3:16). Thus in today's verses, members of John's faithful community are rightfully called children
of God because they accepted Jesus (John 1:10-12), while the
Secessionists (the world, or Israelites who did not accept
Jesus) refused to recognize their fellow Israelites as children of
God because they refused to recognize Jesus as Son. (The
Greek word *teknon* is a technical Johannine term for describing divine sonship or daughtership; son *[huios]* is reserved for
Jesus' relationship to God.) In the end, the fullness of the be-
lievers' identity will be revealed. They will realize that they are
like God, for everyone will see God clearly.

The polemics of the Secessionists have raised doubts in the
community. Their argument is: if behavior is as important as
you say it is, how do you know that you have not sinned, or if
you have sinned, how can you be certain you are forgiven? The
sacred author counters this by saying if we do what is pleasing
to God (keep his commandments, especially to love the
brethren), God will do what is pleasing to us (our petitions are
answered). The Johannine commandment is to believe in Jesus
and to love one another (v. 23, in contrast to the synoptic tradition Mark 12:28-31 and parallels). To believe in Jesus is to
have faith in God whose Son Jesus is and who has sent Jesus to
us. The believers' response is to love the brethren and the result
is intimate union with God. This emphasis on Jesus incarnate is
yet another counter-offensive to the Secessionists who denied
Jesus in the flesh. Today's gospel (Luke 2:41-52) relating the
anxiety Jesus caused Joseph and Mary with his five-day separa-
tion from them demonstrates just how very "human" he was,
and what a typically human, Mediterranean family he had.

January 1:
Octave Day of Christmas:
Solemnity of the Blessed Virgin Mary, The Mother of God
Galatians 4:4-7

[For background to this letter, see Ninth Sunday in Ordinary Time.] For Paul, the advent of Jesus marked the beginning of a new "time." Specifically, it was the redemptive death of Jesus that formed the dividing line signaling the end of one age and the beginning of another (then–now; once–but now). Jesus was born an Israelite and circumcised, hence he became subject to the law (then). But his death abrogated the covenant of law and established a new covenant of faith and grace (now; Gal 3:13-14). In his own life, Jesus manifests the precise pattern of the covenant of faith, its significance, and how it works in day-to-day life. Jesus is the unique "son" that God promised to Abraham (Gal 3:16), thus becoming a model for whoever would be son (or daughter) with God (Gal 4:5-7). This defines the status of any and every believer. Just as Jesus prayed to his Abba (Mark 14:36, the only place this word appears in the Gospels), so his followers are filled with the Spirit and pray as he did: "Abba, Father" (Gal 4:6).

It is probably unnecessary but still helpful to remind ourselves that the Aramaic word "Abba" never meant "Daddy," but rather exactly as reported in the Greek of Mark meant and was understood as "Father." Even in the English language, there is a difference between "Father" and "Daddy." In 1988, James Barr reviewed the linguistic evidence and noted that in its cultural context, that is, the ancient Israelite social system, Abba was a term of formal address. It was not used as a familiar, intimate, warm, and loving term (see Pilch 1999: 1–3). The significance for these passages (Mark and Galatians) is that now after the death of Jesus, his followers have the same relationship to God that Jesus had. God is Father to his believers. That is indeed good news. The term, however, fits well into the Mediterranean cultural matrix where love for the father is always demonstrated in a respectful way. In this culture, the son is not the father's equal or "pal." As reflected in Sirach (3:6-7), the culture notes that "he who fears the LORD honors his father, / and serves his parents as rulers."

Luke (2:16-21) depicts the way in which Jesus was indeed subject to his parents from the very beginning. He was circumcised on the eighth day and given the name assigned by the angel. The pattern of his life lived faithfully under the law helps to appreciate the new relationship with God that Jesus made possible for all, Israelite and non-Israelite alike.

Second Sunday after Christmas
Ephesians 1:3-6, 15-18

Contemporary scholarly opinion lists this letter among the Deutero-Paulines, that is, it was likely written after Paul's death by disciples sometime between A.D. 80 and 100. These verses from a letter in the Pauline tradition are part of the customary blessing (vv. 3-14) and thanksgiving (vv. 15-23) sections which begin most of the letters. Why should we bless God? Primarily because God chose us in Jesus just as he chose special people before us (see Deut 14:2). Given the gratuitous nature of God's choice, one can only marvel and be grateful. Of course, that election involves an obligation: God's chosen people must be holy and without blemish in God's presence. Yet another reason for requiring such holiness and purity is that the Ephesian congregation, like the Colossian congregation, was convinced that angels were in the midst of the worshiping community (see Eph 3:10; also 2:6). This is similar to the sentiments at Qumran where anyone physically blemished "shall not enter to take their place among the congregation of famous men, for the angels of holiness are among their congregation" (1QSa 2:8-9).

God has not just chosen us but also adopted us. Scholars observe that in this culture where family (kinship) is one of the dominant social institutions and is rather extensive and complex, there was no mechanism for adoption. That Paul can conclude that God adopts us is an interesting breakthrough. Those who heard this from Paul and his circle would be awed. God's election bestows incredible honor and far-reaching consequences.

The thanksgiving section (vv. 15-18) appears to have been patterned after Phlm 4-5. Paul prays that they may receive wisdom and revelation so that they may come to know God even better. Wisdom in the Bible involves practical or experiential knowledge and the ability to choose proper conduct. In Paul, wisdom often involved understanding more clearly God's activity in Jesus and the benefits believers receive from such knowledge. The upshot of Paul's prayer is that the Ephesians might appreciate the immense privileges that God has bestowed upon them.

The gospel for today (John 1:1-18) talks about the Word who literally in Greek "pitched his tent among us" (v. 14). Those who received him were empowered to become "children of God" (v. 12). The Ephesian verses provide still further information about the truly blessed condition of being adopted by God. No doubt all modern believers can readily repeat Paul's prayer that they, too, might understand and appreciate the astounding honor of being so chosen by God. How amazing is this God!

January 6: Epiphany
Ephesians 3:2-3a, 5-6

This letter was probably written by a disciple of Paul between 80–100 A.D. The author repeats Paul's great insight here, that non-Israelites (Gentiles) have full and co-equal membership with Israelites in the Church through Christ Jesus. In the Greek texts three adjectives with the prefix syn- (together) make this point emphatically (co-heirs, co-members, co-partners, v. 6). Actually, the insight results from a direct revelation from God (compare Gal 1:12, 16) which by this time in the tradition has become normative. Given the history of the chosen people, the covenant, and related concepts, only God could have revealed that the divine will now include non-Israelites in that people. This idea would be too preposterous for any human being to initiate on personal initiative.

Another interesting point is that this revelation/insight has been given to "holy apostles and prophets" (v. 5). Scholars remind us that Paul (e.g., in Galatians 1–2) insisted that he alone received the distinctive revelation concerning the place of non-Israelites in the Church. That the author of Ephesians now extends it to others (apostles and prophets) is a strong argument that this is an author writing in the name of Paul, and not Paul himself.

The common link between this reading and the gospel for today's feast (Matt 2:1-12) is the Magi, non-Israelites who come to do homage to Jesus at his birth. In Romans, Paul makes the boldest statement of his understanding of the relationship of non-Israelites to Israelites by calling the grafting of non-Israelites to Israelites "unnatural" or "contrary to nature" (Rom 11:24). Only a revelation from God could convince humans that this is the divine will. Contemporary church members who are overwhelmingly of non-Israelite lineage should be awed by God's decision. Today's feast provides an opportunity to formulate a convincing reply to a question frequently asked by outsiders: "Knowing the history of the Church and its warts, why do you remain a Christian?"

Baptism of the Lord
(First Sunday in Ordinary Time)
Titus 2:11-14; 3:4-7

[See Christmas Midnight Mass and Mass at Dawn. For background to the Pastorals see Twenty-Fourth Sunday in Ordinary Time.] This letter (along with 1 and 2 Timothy) has been dubbed by tradition as one of the Pastoral epistles. They have been called Pastoral epistles since the eighteenth century because they are addressed to "pastors" of early communities. For this reason, the anonymous person who wrote this letter under the name of Paul, who was already dead, is usually called "the Pastor."

The architects of the lectionary have omitted the first and very important word in today's reading: "for." In Greek this particle always points backwards. The verses that follow this word provide the motive for what preceded (vv. 1-10 are guidelines for behavior based on age and gender: older men/older women; younger men/younger women). Thus have the architects made these verses somewhat "free floating" in the liturgy.

The key word now is "appeared" (v. 11), and its tense in Greek signals a once-and-for-always perspective. How has the grace of God appeared once-and-for-always? The noun "appearance" occurs just six times in the New Testament and always in reference to Jesus. So the process by which God relates to humans (= "grace") has been revealed once and forever in Jesus, in what he said and did and means for us (= salvation).

What is God doing for us? "Training us," that is, forming us as authentic human beings in all respects: emotionally, intellectually, socially, religiously, politically, and any other way we might imagine. In modern terms, God is relating to us now holistically.

How does God train us? We must (a) reject godless ways and (b) worldly desires. Instead, on the positive side we must live (b') temperately, justly, and (a') devoutly. Notice the arrangement of ideas, so common in the Bible (a, b, b', a'). Godless ways would be equivalent to religious indifferentism or atheistic secularism. If science or some other idol usurps God's role to be in charge of life, the result is a godless way of life.

Worldly desires might be interpreted as accepting the dictates of one's culture without critical evaluation. Many people in Western culture derive a sense of self-worth from having a job or the right kind of job. Does human worth and identity depend on a job, or on something other than one's job? Instead, believers are called to lead sensible, self-controlled lives and to live justly or uprightly. This means one must live in good interpersonal relationships with other human beings. Finally, to live devoutly is to acknowledge God's reign in our personal lives. While this may sound like excessive reliance upon personal efforts, the Pastor says exactly the opposite: it is God's grace that makes good living possible. God's activity on our behalf through Jesus makes us true human beings. Moreover, God's training is effective because of Jesus' voluntary death in total obedience to the Father so that we might be cleansed and eager to do good.

Scholars recognize Titus 3:4-7 as a popular "creed" which the Pastor inserted at this point in his letter as a comment on good deeds (3:1, 5, 8) and bad deeds (3:9). (Examples of other such creedal statements in the Pastorals would be 1 Tim 1:15; 2:4-6; 3:16; 6:12-16; 2 Tim 1:8-10; Titus 2:11-14.) Such creedal statements may have originated in the context of liturgies. If so, the Pastor's ready reliance on creeds in his instructions about proper behavior (good and bad deeds) is an excellent example of moving from liturgy to life among our ancestors in the faith.

The Pastor's creed-based observation is that good deeds by themselves don't merit anything from God (v. 5). Rather, everything is a free gift coming to us through baptism. But remember that in Mediterranean culture, there really are no free gifts. Every gift expects one in return, or at least some kind of response. This response is "good deeds."

Today's gospel (Luke 3:15-16, 21-22) reports the baptism of Jesus, the incarnate appearance of the grace of God for the people who "were filled with expectation." The more deeply believers come to know who Jesus is, the more incumbent it is upon them to lead lives filled with good deeds.

Second Sunday in Ordinary Time
1 Corinthians 12:4-11

Paul wrote this letter from Ephesus about the year 54 A.D. This segment of 1 Corinthians extending to 14:40 is Paul's response to questions about "spiritual gifts" or "charisms" (Greek: *charismata*). A charism is the manifestation in an individual person of God's grace *(charis)* which came through Jesus the Messiah and which is expressed through service. When there is no more need for that service, the charism is ended. In other words, God calls individuals to service (or ministry) within the community and provides the ability to fulfill that service or ministry.

Every Christian has her or his own charism: "to each individual the manifestation of the spirit is given for some benefit" (1 Cor 12:7; see also 3:5; 11:18; Rom 12:3). No charism is better or superior. All are valuable. Variety is the word here. In Paul's day some of the more common charisms were communication (apostles, prophets, teachers, et al.), social service (deacons and deaconesses, those tending the sick and poor, almsgivers, et al.), and executive positions (overseers [bishops], shepherds [pastors], elders, et al.). Notice that the charism is to be used for and with others; it is not a personal mark of privilege or prestige. As Paul tells us later (1 Corinthians 13), the most excellent charism is love (agape).

In today's verses, the gifts or charisms have a common source; hence, they should be used in service of the common good. The listing in vv. 8-10 is just a sample. It is not intended to be an exhaustive list. Many more examples could be given but such lists are usually limited to ten items (though this one seems to have only nine). Precise definitions of these gifts are difficult because we do not know exactly how the Corinthians understood them. Be that as it may, Paul's conclusion is critical. The Spirit is responsible for the gifts and their diversity. It is the Spirit that distributes them to individuals who therefore have no basis for feeling proud or taking any credit. The recipient's chief obligation is to use the gifts in service of others.

At Cana (John 2:1-11), Jesus used his particular gift not just to spare the groom from the shame of running out of wine, but to serve those attending the wedding so that their joy might be full and complete according to the cultural expectations. In the context of contemporary interest in diversity within Western culture, today's readings provide an opportunity to reflect upon the Spirit who gives different gifts to individuals according to the divine will so that they might use these diverse gifts to serve others.

Third Sunday in Ordinary Time
1 Corinthians 12:12-30

From the fifth century B.C. until the sixth century A.D., the most prominent healing god in the Mediterranean world was Asclepius. When the pilgrims who visited his shrines were healed, they left behind a memento in the shape of the healed body-part inscribed with the ailment, the remedy recommended by Asclepius in a dream, and the result. There was such a healing shrine in Corinth which might have inspired Paul with the idea to symbolize believers as parts of the body of Christ. (Modern visitors to Corinth can see echoes of these mementos reflected the Orthodox tradition in St. George chapel atop Mount Lykabettos, the highest hill of Athens. Here healed people have left similar tokens.)

Paul dwells on this image of the body at some length. He speaks of the body of Christ, by which he means the Church. It is a holy body because it is filled with a holy spirit (3:16; 6:19). But it must also be whole, that is, exist without dissension, factions, and divisions. As wholeness indicates the purity of the physical body, so unity reveals the holiness of the social body.

Bodily defect and mutilation threaten the physical body. Dissension, divisions, factions threaten the social body. The Corinthians have broken into factions (Paul, Apollos, Cephas, Christ—1:12; 3:4). There are divisions between strong and weak (1:18-29), wise and foolish (8:10-13), and the like.

Today's verses indicate that the threats are within the body of Christ. Two different sets of anatomical parts speak in 12:15-16 and 21. The first set feel inferior and not welcome in the body (foot because it is not a hand; ear because it is not an eye). The second set feel superior and boast that it alone is the only part of the body that is honorable (the eye is superior to the hand; the head to the feet). Both postures threaten the wholeness of the physical body, and the unity of the social body. Feelings of inferiority make a member feel like an outsider to the group. Superiority complexes foster individualism and elitism and humiliate others. Paul's point is that God has ordained the body parts as they are. This is how things ought to be.

Then Paul ranks the body parts as honorable and less honorable, presentable and inferior, stronger and weaker. This ranking relates to the different roles ascribed to members of the Church: apostles, prophets, etc. This, too, is God's doing, this is what "God has designated." In other words, the threat to the body of Christ, in Paul's view, is individualism, perhaps an exaggerated form of it. He proposes instead a commitment to group orientation, to seeking the well-being of others. His concern is "that there may be no division in the body, but that parts may have the same concern for one another."

Luke reports how Jesus read from the Isaiah scroll and interpreted the Scripture for his fellow villagers (Luke 4:14-21). He also introduces himself as an author who had written and interpreted the results of his investigations (Luke 1:1-4). Paul offered the Corinthians an interpretation of what it means to be community. For Paul, individualism is the enemy of community. Modern Western believers who cherish individualism as a core value may not welcome Paul's exhortation to temper individualism in the interests of the social body, the Church. If the preachers have made the challenge of today's Scriptures clear and sharp, Western participants in the liturgy will have much to consider.

Fourth Sunday in Ordinary Time
1 Corinthians 12:31–13:13

In these verses, Paul describes for the Corinthians a more excellent way, the most excellent charism (or spiritual gift): agape or love. He uses the same literary form that he used earlier (see Second Sunday in Ordinary Time, above: 1 Cor 12:4-11). In describing love he lists ten examples. The list is not intended to be exhaustive.

Patience is courage but exercised always out of consideration for others. To be kind is to be open-handed and open-hearted. Jealous is better translated as envious, which would bring in the Middle Eastern concept of evil-eye: one should not cast the evil eye toward others, that is, persecute or make life miserable for them. It is rude or inconsiderate to put others down through boastful pride. In this culture, seeking one's own interests must always occur at the expense of others. Honor is a zero sum game: if one gains, someone else loses. A quick temper results in anger, which could escalate to violence, perhaps even bloodshed resulting in a generations-long blood-feud. Instead of brooding over injury, one must forgive and forget. Evil deeds happening to others should not cause rejoicing; rather, the revelation of God's plan (truth) should be the reason for rejoicing.

Notice how prominent "others" are in this explanation of love (vv. 4-7). The introductory contrasts (vv. 1-3) focus on individual gifts (tongues, prophecy, self-despoilment), which amount to nothing if they are not directed to the benefit of others. The concluding antitheses (vv. 8-13: never–at some time; in part–entirely; child–adult; now–then; three–best of all) underline the excellence and permanence of love.

What, then, is the love Paul describes? It is a way of life expressed in observable conduct that proceeds from an internal personal quality or divine force. It is possible for human beings to love like this at all only because God loved human beings first (1 Cor 8:3; 13:12–the passive voice "fully known" is a theological passive: God has known and loved us first). Once aware of what God did and continues to do for us, human beings have no choice but to love others. Moreover, in Mediterranean culture, these final three items bear a distinctive meaning. Faith is loyalty, or sticking with another no matter what. Hope is trust, or putting all one's eggs in the other's basket. And love is group-cohesion, absolute commitment to the unity and integrity of the community. This is not humanistic philanthropy, a vague love of humankind. The love Paul describes is directed primarily to neighbor, especially insofar as the neighbor offers difficulty to or for us. To understand this kind of love fully, substitute Jesus for love in vv. 4-7. No wonder, then, that the greatest of all spiritual gifts is love.

In today's gospel (Luke 4:21-30), Jesus' preaching evokes fury from his fellow villagers who want to kill him. But he, loving them, passed through their midst and went away. The reality reported in the gospel urges worshipers to keep in mind that Paul's inspiring poem about love was formulated because of his painful experiences from fellow believers in Corinth. The liturgy reminds us never to lose sight of the challenges to love posed by real-life experiences.

Fifth Sunday in Ordinary Time
1 Corinthians 15:1-11

Scholars agree that at the heart of these verses lies a very old piece of tradition, something that was already "fixed" by the spring A.D. 54 and could not be changed. Paul uses technical terms (in Greek, reflecting the Hebrew) to assure his listeners/readers that he is reporting the tradition verbatim: "I handed on to you" that which "I also received." It is trustworthy. The tradition is in vv. 3b-5: Messiah died, was buried, was raised, and was seen. Then follows a list of those who saw the Risen Jesus.

The importance of such a list is to identify people who have legitimate "ascribed" authority in the community, the Church. By virtue of seeing the Lord, these people receive a specific ascribed role ("Am I not an apostle? Have I not seen Jesus our Lord?" 1 Cor 9:11) with specific rights and duties. Cephas is first on the list either because Jesus appeared to him first (Luke 24:34) or because Jesus confirmed his leadership role among the brethren (Luke 22:31-32; John 21:15-19). Paul is last on the list perhaps because he persecuted believers and is "not fit to be called an apostle."

The important thing about this list is that Paul is on it at all! To judge by what he writes in this letter, the gifted among the Corinthians did not have a high opinion of Paul. They considered him "un-wise," "hardly eloquent," "not a spirit-person," and "weak." Why should anyone pay attention to him? It is very likely for this reason that Paul emphatically insists that although he is "last" in time and "least" among legitimate authorities, he, too, is gifted by God: "By the grace of God I am what I am." This is an honor claim to be included among the other elites and presumably among the gifted members of the church at Corinth. Moreover, in relationship to the others on this list, Paul insists he has "toiled harder than all of them." That is quite an honor claim! But in this culture where honor is the core value, everything rides on one's honor claim and its confirmation by the public.

Some scholars interpret Paul's statement that Jesus showed himself "last of all to me" to mean that no one after this saw the risen Jesus. While this interpretation may be plausible, there is perhaps a still more plausible view rooted in Mediterranean culture. The family is the prevailing model for society, and in the family every member is indispensable. It is unthinkable that the family could be constituted by any other but these members, whatever their level of skill or ability. This is how Paul explains the value of persons with different gifts in the Corinthian community (see the comments above on 1 Corinthians 12 for the Second and Third Sundays in Ordinary Time, Cycle C). By identifying himself among the last of those currently alive to whom Jesus showed himself, Paul becomes an indispensable witness. Making oneself indispensable is typical in Mediterranean cultures. Paul simply wants to make himself indispensable in the surrogate family composed of those who believe in Jesus.

Today's gospel (Luke 5:1-11) reports how Jesus called his first followers who, according to Luke (Acts 1:22), deserved the title apostle because they were with him from the baptism until his ascension. These were indispensable witnesses to the life and ministry of Jesus. Paul acknowledges their authority but includes himself because the risen Jesus also showed himself to Paul. Is there any way in which modern believers can imitate the Mediterranean value of becoming an indispensable witness to the life and ministry of Jesus?

Sixth Sunday in Ordinary Time
1 Corinthians 15:12, 16-20

In order to appreciate Paul's comment on resurrection, it is
necessary to understand the problems he faced in Corinth.
Most likely the spirit- people believed they already possessed
eternal life. (They deduced this from philosophical speculation about wisdom rooted in Philo, a Judean who lived in
Alexandria, Egypt, about 20 B.C. to A.D. 50.) Since they felt
certain of already possessing eternal life, they denied resurrection of the body. Who needs it if eternal life is a present
possession?

After presenting the thesis of his opponents (v. 12), he
draws from it four conclusions: (1) Christ has not been raised;
(2) Paul's preaching misrepresents God; (3) the Corinthians
are still sinners—nothing has changed; (4) those who died as
Christians are fools who are totally lost. If this life is all there
is, "we are the most pitiable people of all."

By suggesting that the thesis of the spirit-people discredits
his preaching, Paul tells them they are in reality not what
they think they are, namely, wise. Paul's preaching stated
that accepting Jesus made a difference in one's life. If Jesus
did not rise, nothing has changed. They are not as "wise" as
they think they are. They are just like the rest of humanity.
By denying the resurrection, the wise have unwittingly destroyed the very basis of their privileged position. Did Paul's
observations hit home? It is difficult to say. Paul concludes

his argument by insisting: Christ has indeed been raised from the dead. What God has done for Jesus can be done for all. He is the "first fruits"; others will follow.

Jesus in today's gospel (Luke 6:17, 20-26) presents a reversal of the honor-code in his culture and assures his seemingly less-than-honorable listeners: "Your reward will be great in heaven." In contrast, the rich, those who are satisfied, and those who are enjoying life now—the "wise"—will see their fortunes reversed. Paul challenges those in Corinth who think they are wise with their denial of the resurrection. The Scriptures for this Sunday should give pause to modern Western believers driven by concerns for relevance, political correctness, and the like. The best way to be relevant is to make sure one really understands the "outdated" or "irrelevant" convictions of our ancestors in the faith.

Seventh Sunday in Ordinary Time
1 Corinthians 15:45-49

In vv. 33-49 Paul answers two questions (in reality, these are doubts formulated by his opponents who deny the resurrection): "What is the nature of the resurrected body?" (vv. 33-44a) and "Does such a body really exist?" (vv. 44b-49). Just as similar-looking seeds produce different plants, so the physical body (like a seed that looks similar to other seeds) rises as a spiritual body, that is, one transformed by the Spirit to a new mode of existence.

To address the second question, Paul relies on principles familiar to and accepted by his opponents. Philo (about 20 B.C. to A.D. 50), a Judean philosopher who lived in Alexandria, taught that the creature of Genesis 1 was a "heavenly" man, and that of Genesis 2 an "earthly" man who was a replica of the heavenly man. For Philo, the first man was incorporeal and incorruptible. Accepting Philo's premise about the two men, Paul changes the interpretation. In v. 45, he cites Gen 2:7b (about the "second" man), "and man became a living being," but adds two key words: "first" and "Adam." For Paul, this second man is now "first" and is clearly a recipient of life. He continues, "the spiritual was not first," but rather the natural. "The first man was from earth, earthly."

What will the last Adam be? This allows Paul to introduce another principle well known in Judaic speculation: the end will correspond with the beginning. Just as it was in the beginning, so will it be in the end. "The second man [is] from heaven," writes Paul. According to Judaic tradition, the last righteous person (the last Adam) will bring out the first man. Paul makes Jesus the last Adam, and in contrast to the first Adam who was a recipient of life, Jesus is a life-giving spirit. The first man began as a righteous being, but fell. The last man completes the return to righteousness. The conclusion: just as we are descendants of the earthly man, we also have the potential to become what the heavenly man is and to have the same sort of body. In the very beginning, that body was incorporeal and incorruptible.

In today's gospel (Luke 6:27-28), Luke's Jesus contrasts the behavior expected of those who follow him with the behavior of "sinners" (in this instance, those who are not following him but pursuing a different lifestyle). This contrast echoes Paul's contrast of the earthly and the heavenly Adam. Admittedly, it is difficult to link these readings. Yet one thought worth pondering is that contemporary believers face the option of continuing after the pattern of the earthly (fallen) Adam, or choosing the quality and direction of the life of the last Adam, Jesus. It was, after all, that lifestyle that won for him resurrection after dying a criminal's death.

Eighth Sunday in Ordinary Time
1 Corinthians 15:54-58

Bringing his reflections on resurrection to a close, Paul emphatically affirms: "But thanks be to God who gives us the
victory through our Lord Jesus Christ" (v. 57). This verse is
familiar from Handel's Messiah in which the composer gave
it a beautifully comforting musical setting. Paul, who lived
centuries before Handel, demonstrates his own peculiar creativity in the way he has refashioned the Scripture he quotes.
Paul combines Isa 25:8 and Hos 13:14. Isaiah says the Lord
"will swallow up death for ever," and Hosea cries, "Where
are your plagues, O death! Where is your sting, O nether
world!" In Hosea's context, however, the phrases are bad
news rather than good news. As the next part of the verse
makes very clear, Hosea reports God's determination to de-
stroy Israel: "My eyes are closed to compassion." Paul has
completely reversed Hosea's intended meaning.

In general, Paul seems to follow rabbinical methods of interpreting Scripture in which this strategy is perfectly acceptable. We who live in the post-enlightenment era are
committed to historical critical principles of reading and interpreting Scripture. According to these principles, we strive
to discover what a sacred author wrote and what that author
actually intended. This method reveals to us what Hosea
wrote and intended, and how Paul has dealt with his tradition. Paul's intended message is quite clear. It is the exact opposite of what Hosea meant.

Appealing as it may be, Paul's method of interpreting Scripture is not a model for modern believers to imitate. Church guidelines and the principles of scientific scholarship insist that until the reader knows what the Scripture meant to its original recipients, it is impossible to determine what it means for the modern reader. According to these guidelines and principles, modern readers are not free to make the Bible say whatever they want it to say, or would prefer that it said. Once the intention and meaning of the original author, like Paul, is determined, the reader must then build a cross-cultural bridge back to a very different, modern world, to discover what its application might be.

Paul exhorts his original audience (and the modern audience) to remain "firm, steadfast, always fully devoted to the work of the Lord." The advice is based on the preceding examination of challenges to and doubts about the resurrection (1 Corinthians 15). The doubts and challenges in the modern world are different from those in Paul's world. Like Paul, modern believers must become intimately familiar with the tradition in order to fashion appropriate responses while remaining faithful to that tradition.

In today's gospel, Luke's Jesus observes: "No disciple is superior to the teacher; but when fully trained, every disciple will be like the teacher" (6:40). The contemporary context challenges modern believers to exercise informed creativity as they reflect upon and seek to draw appropriate applications to modern life from their ancient Mediterranean traditions.

Ninth Sunday in Ordinary Time
Galatians 1:1-2, 6-10

The circumstances which prompted Paul to write this letter from Ephesus about the year A.D. 54 obviously made him very angry. He begins his letter with an uncharacteristically strong declaration of his authority as an apostle. All his letters, but Galatians in particular, indicate that Paul lived in tension and rivalry with other leaders because of disorderly competition for leadership. A number of factors come into play here. Everyone knew Paul was not one of the Twelve. He wouldn't even qualify according to the requirements spelled out by Luke (Acts 1:21-22). Paul, on the contrary, insisted that his role as apostle was not a self-designation but an appointment by God.

From a cultural perspective, another set of factors enters the picture. Paul (perhaps with the fellow believers who are with him) founded these churches to whom the letter is addressed. Thus Paul is making a powerful appeal to the loyalty he has a right to expect from them. This letter indicates that their loyalty has seriously lapsed. Paul seeks to reactivate their emotionally anchored commitment to God's activity in Jesus ("raised him from the dead," v. 1) and to the gospel Paul preached to them (v. 9). In the Mediterranean world, loyalty once activated is expected to be life-long.

This expectation helps understand the next verses in today's reading (6-10). Customarily at this point in a letter, Paul would offer a prayer of thanksgiving for the letter recipients (e.g., 1 Thess 1:2-10). Here Paul omits a thanksgiving senti-ment. Instead, he deliberately and forcefully seeks to shame the Galatians for switching allegiance from him and the gospel he preached to another message. The mention of an "angel from heaven" (v. 8) presenting a gospel different from Paul's helps identify the culprits as Judaizers. An Israelite tradition believed that angels enacted the Mosaic Law. Those preaching another gospel are proposing that those accepting Jesus as Messiah should also observe Judaic ritual practices such as circumcision and dietary restrictions.

Paul's ultimate argument is to curse these people. People in Mediterranean cultures understand the power of words. Once spoken, words cannot be retracted. A curse pronounced is a curse put into effect. This is similar to the insult Jesus hurled against Chorazin, Bethsaida, and Capernaum when he com-pared them to non-Israelite and thoroughly inhospitable populations and judged these three to be worse (Luke 10:13)! Middle Eastern listeners would be stunned and frightened by such curses and insults.

In today's gospel (Luke 7:1-10), Jesus marvels at the de-gree of loyalty ("such faith," v. 9) he experienced in a non-Israelite (centurion) which was totally lacking in Israel! Loyalty, sticking with someone or some conviction no mat-ter what, is a paramount value among our ancestors in the faith. Western loyalty tends to be pragmatic, depending upon "what's in it for me?" Would Jesus and Paul bless us, or insult and curse us?

Tenth Sunday in Ordinary Time
Galatians 1:11-19

It is noteworthy that Paul uses the same Greek word here to introduce his explanation of how he learned the gospel (from God alone) and in 1 Corinthians to introduce a fragment of tradition he "received" from human sources (1 Cor 15:1): "I want you to know." The two instances, however, are dramatically different. In the latter case, Paul learned, memorized, and faithfully handed on a tradition about death and resurrection of Jesus. In today's verses, his emphatic point is that he learned the gospel he preaches from God and not from any human source.

Observe Paul's use of a major Middle Eastern cultural technique in interpersonal relations. In the five chapters of this letter, he repeats the word "brothers" (inclusive language translations add "sisters") eleven times. These are not Paul's blood relatives, but the phrase reminds the audience that they have become "as if" they were so related by reason of believing in Jesus and living by the gospel Paul preached to them. Repetition of this kinship terminology is a conversational glue intended to keep bonding the speaker/writer and the audience ever closer together. This is the style Paul typically uses to assert his authority.

By alluding to Jeremiah (1:5) and Isaiah (42:1), Paul presents himself as standing in the same prophetic tradition. Just as God selected them, so did God choose Paul for a special task. After revealing to Paul Jesus' true identity (son),

God commissioned him to tell the good news about Jesus to the non-Israelite world. Paul's response poses quite a challenge to believers in any age: it was immediate, unquestioning, and intense. He didn't "double-check" with others or pause to make a retreat and discern a course of action. He went straight to work in the region west and south of Judea known as the Nabatean Kingdom.

The last two verses (18-19) seem to contradict what preceded. Paul claims he received the gospel directly from God, yet now he goes to Jerusalem "to confer with" Cephas for two weeks. It is important to remember that Paul and Cephas were collectivistic personalities, that is, they were embedded in groups and derived their identity and significance from these groups. The troubles in Galatia erupted when Paul's converts as a group began switching loyalty from Paul and the gospel he preached to the Judaizing preachers and their "gospel." The Judaizers insisted their views were more in tune with Jerusalem than Paul's views. Paul seeks to align himself and his message with the Jerusalem group. He presents himself as Peter's equal (this would strengthen Paul's insistence on his identity as an apostle). At the same time, it is very plausible that Cephas shared with Paul his experiences during Jesus' ministry.

In that ministry as reported today by Luke (7:11-17), people said of Jesus: "A great prophet has arisen in our midst." In writing to the Galatians, Paul claimed for himself the same identity, prophet, that is, a spokesperson for God telling God's will for the here and now. A modern believer could wish for no better minister.

First Sunday of Lent
Romans 10:8-13

The anti-introspective Israelites made judgments on the basis of external criteria, chiefly, the human body viewed in three symbolic segments: heart-eyes (the seat of emotion-fused thought), mouth-ears (the zone of self-expressive speech), and hands-feet (the zone of purposeful activity). A sick person usually ailed in one or another zone. People who emphasized one zone more than the other ought to seek a balance between all three. (Notice which zone is not represented in Jesus' critique of Pharisee behaviors in Matt 6:1-18.)

Today's verses are part of the unit extending from v. 1 to v. 13, the central point of which is that "Christ is the end of the law for the justification of everyone who has faith" (v. 4). One becomes right with God by faith rather than by human efforts. "Works of the law" are performed by the hands-feet symbolic body zone. Faith is centered in the heart-eyes and mouth-ears zones. If you confess with your mouth (mouth-ears) and believe in your heart (heart-eyes) that Jesus is Lord and that God raised him from the dead, you will be saved. Paul draws on and modifies two statements from Israelite tradition to confirm his statement: "No one who believes in him will be put to shame" (Isa 28:16, a heart-eyes passage) and "everyone who calls on the name of the Lord will be saved" (Joel 3:5, a mouth-ears passage). It is a very clever, culturally appropriate way of putting "hands-feet" in proper perspective and of putting emphasis on the universality of God's good will (no distinction . . . everyone!).

Second Sunday of Lent
Philippians 3:17–4:1

These verses are from Letter B (or C) to the Philippians (see Introductory comments above, Second Sunday in Advent). Itinerant missionaries, undoubtedly well intended but quite misguided according to Paul's standards, have visited the Philippians and urged them to adopt Judaic ritual practices which Paul no longer includes as behaviors required of believers in Jesus Messiah. These might include Israelite dietary rules (Leviticus 11) but definitely do include circumcision ("shame" is a euphemism for the male sex organ in v. 19). If dietary rules are Paul's concern, he may have learned of Peter's vision in which God instructed Peter that all foods are clean (Acts 10:15-16, with Peter's new understanding in 11:1-18). Why do some believers insist on resisting God? Why do they make their stomach into a God? But scholars think that there is a more plausible referent for "their god is the belly" (v. 19). The Greek translation of the Bible (LXX) frequently uses this word (belly) to denote affections, the mind, the innermost heart, the person; in other words, self-esteem. This would suggest a better translation: "their god is self-esteem."

In v. 20 Paul again uses citizenship language: "our citizenship is in heaven." His use of political language and rhetoric in these verses as he responds to behavior with which he disagrees suggests that Philippian believers are being harassed for political reasons and are beginning to question their suffering. Why should they suffer shame from neighbors when awards of honor would be so much easier to win? Their self-esteem is at stake! What harm would come from compromising and fulfilling the civic duties of participating in the emperor cult, thus preserving self-esteem?

With regard to their intention of reinstating circumcision, Paul resorts to insult, a common Middle Eastern cultural strategy in conflict over honor. They take their honor, Paul says, from mutilating the male sex organ, for which we all know the Hebrew euphemism: "shame." One can almost hear the community join Paul in sarcastic laughter: they take honor in shame!

The principle difficulty with the opponents' position is that it makes them enemies of the cross of the Messiah. By insisting on circumcision of non-Israelite believers in Messiah Jesus, these preachers deny what Jesus' death on the cross accomplished. They make void the sacrifice of Jesus. It brings Paul to tears, and such a display of emotion is quite natural and spontaneous among Middle Eastern men. It is very likely not literary hyperbole. Those in the community who have wavered or been swayed by the itinerant preachers should follow the example of Paul and others. It was common for teachers to exhort disciples to imitate and share in their striving for perfection. Thus Paul's exhortation: "Stand firm!" (4:1) as he has. At the parousia the real savior, Jesus (not Nero) will act as Lord.

The voice from heaven (God) in today's gospel (Luke 9:28b-36) tells the disciples: "THIS [Jesus] is my chosen son; listen to HIM . . . [more so than to Moses and Elijah, his conversation partners in the trance]." Effectively, Paul gives the same advice to the Philippians: "Understand and appreciate the significance of Messiah's redeeming death. . . . Don't revert to those ritual practices now rendered unnecessary and thereby deny the value of Jesus' death and God's salvific will." Can modern believers follow the example of Paul and say to others: "Become imitators of me, conduct yourself according to the model you have in me and others who imitate me"?

Third Sunday of Lent
1 Corinthians 10:1-6, 10-12

The main point of this reading is a warning against being overconfident. "Whoever thinks he is standing secure, should take care not to fall" (v. 12). The vehicle for proclaiming this warning is a reflection on baptism. So far as we know, Paul does not seem to have presided at this ritual very often (1 Cor 1:14-17). By definition, a ritual is an action that moves a person from one state of being to a new state of being. This, of course, is what baptism accomplishes. The candidate separates her or himself from the old, then participates in a ritual of immersion, and emerges from the pool of water into a new state of being.

Paul presumes his audience knows well the Exodus narrative. He alludes to it in the first five verses and follows the sequence of Exodus carefully: the cloud (Exod 13:21), the sea (14:21), the manna (16:4, 14-18), the water (17:6), and the rebellion (32:6). Paul's comment on these events is significant (1 Cor 10:6). The lectionary translation reads thus: "these things happened as examples for us." A more literal translation would be: "these things were types of us." The Greek word behind "types" reflects Paul's interpretation of Exodus in a "typical" sense, a style of interpretation very popular among the Fathers of the Church. The typical sense presumes that there is a deeper meaning of Scripture when it seems to have foreshadowed future elements in God's work of salvation. In today's verses, we see Paul's "creative" mind at work when he refers to our ancestors as "baptized into Moses." This, of course, is reading a Christian ritual back into a pre-Christian event (Exodus).

Paul's connection of the two events (Exodus and baptism) has become an integral part of our understanding. Still, the connection highlights the difficulty of this kind of interpretation. How does one know the events are related this way in God's plan? How does one separate that relationship from those constructed by the creative imagination of the contemporary reader or interpreter? Although the role of "typology" is still appreciated, this perspective in contemporary Bible interpretation has been included in considerations of metaphor and symbol in literary criticism.

In light of this consideration, what can be said of the lectionary translation? Are these events "examples for us," or would you prefer "types of us"? Does it make a difference? What difference would it make? In today's gospel (Luke 13:1-9), Jesus alludes to two historical events and urges repentance before the unexpected happens and catches you unaware. That too is a caution against overconfidence. He concludes by telling a parable. How would you relate a "parable" to a "type" or "example"?

Fourth Sunday of Lent
2 Corinthians 5:17-21

In the biblical world, sin basically is an action that shames another person, whether human or divine. In Mediterranean culture, shame requires vengeance. The shamed person has a right and duty to seek redress, to restore the honor that has been besmirched. Paul, however, reminds the Corinthians that the cultural world has been dramatically reshaped (old things passed away, new things have come). Almost straining credulity, Paul insists God has worked this change.

Human beings who have sinned against God have shamed God. God is justified in seeking redress (see Leviticus 26 for an example of how God seeks redress when Israel sins). Jesus, however, through God's decision (Rom 8:3) accepts a relationship to God which normally derives only from sin. Jesus takes on the responsibility of sinners. Through God's loving action in Jesus, then, all humans receive forgiveness of sin, that is, forgiveness for having shamed God and thereby become reconciled with God.

In typical Mediterranean cultural understanding, however, the good graces of the patron (God) become available to clients (sinners) through brokers (ambassadors for Jesus Messiah). Ambassadors, like Paul, made the saving action of Jesus real and available to their contemporaries. Paul begs the Corinthians to be reconciled to God, as all such ministers implore their contemporaries to become reconciled to God.

Today's gospel (Luke 15:1-3, 11-32) so familiar to believers can also be read from the perspective of reconciliation.

God is willing to reconcile the deliberately malicious and the ostensibly righteous to peace and harmonious living. A broker, like Paul, might have helped the elder, apparently resistant son.

Fifth Sunday of Lent
Philippians 3:8-14

[For background, see Second Sunday of Advent.] Like the prophets with whom he associated himself (Jeremiah, Isaiah, see Gal 1:15), Paul speaks forthrightly, clearly, and sometimes in earthy fashion. The Greek word translated "loss" often means "excrement" and may well be Paul's intention in v. 8. Compared to the transforming personal experience of Jesus my Lord, everything else is excrement. Just prior to these verses, Paul presented himself as an unparalleled observer of the tradition: circumcised, an Israelite of the tribe of Benjamin, a Pharisee, a persecutor of deviants who rejected the tradition (vv. 4-5). But Paul realized the Law offered no remedy for sin but led rather to death. The Law was not the way to righteousness offered by God in Messiah Jesus who made possible for all a renewed relationship with God. Thus Paul cries out: "all my accomplishments of which I boasted, I now consider to be rubbish, garbage, loss, excrement."

Paul just wants to know (= experience) Messiah Jesus as a life-giving spirit (2 Cor 3:17). This is how believers in the here-and-now do battle with and conquer the forces of death in preparation for resurrection. According to Paul, the more closely one shares in Jesus' sufferings and becomes conformed to his death, the more certain one can be of traveling on the right path that leads to resurrection.

The image Paul uses to make his point is an athletic event, a race. The runner presses forward forgetting what was passed and focusing only on what still remains to be done. The winner can expect the "upward calling" by God to receive the reward, nothing less than life eternal with God in Messiah Jesus. (Upward calling is an allusion to the ritual in games where the winner was called to step up on the platform to receive the prize.)

The woman caught in adultery (John 8:1-11) had no recourse against her accusers who, like Paul, excelled in knowledge and practice of the law. The cleverness of Jesus in responding to the challenge of these experts won the woman an acquittal from them and from him. This illustrated the graciousness of God at work in Jesus which would become available to all through his death and resurrection. Should one rely on human effort and accomplishment or on God's graciousness? How could the choice be more obvious?

Palm Sunday
of the Lord's Passion
Philippians 2:6-11

Intra-community squabbles about how to live the Gospel threatened to divide the Philippians. Paul exhorts them to put aside differences, close ranks, and pursue the virtue of humility after the pattern of Jesus (vv. 1-5). Then, in this well-known hymn (vv. 6-11), Paul presents Jesus as a model for the Philippians to imitate. Scholars agree that this hymn was composed prior to and independently of this letter. It has two sections: vv. 6-8 describe Jesus' humiliation (a shameful thing in this culture); while vv. 9-11 tell how God exalted him to unimaginable honor. Paul uses this hymn to exert moral pressure on the Philippians.

Many commentators see in v. 6 an implicit contrast between Adam, who wanted to exploit likeness to God for selfish purposes, and Jesus, who did not. The verses contain many allusions to Genesis 1–3. In the Israelite tradition, being godlike means being immune from death (Wis 2:23). These verses compare the human Jesus with the human Adam (it is not a reference to preexistent Jesus who became human). They contrast Jesus' refusal as the final Adam to seek equality with God but highlight his humility and obedience to God in accepting mortality with the first Adam's arrogance and disobedience. He sought to be equal to God as immortal, disobeyed God, and was cursed by God.

By his shameful death, Jesus was humiliated, a major tragedy in this honor driven culture. But God loved Jesus and exalted him. Thus the basic meaning of Jesus died and was raised is that he was humiliated and exalted, by God of course. The phrase "on the cross" disturbs the poetry of the hymn and was very likely added by Paul to underscore the degree of Jesus' humiliation. In response (vv. 9-11), God exalted Jesus to rule over the entire universe. Jesus is Lord, the same word used in the Greek Bible to be spoken instead of YHWH. The one who in total obedience took on the low rank of slave now by God's own commission is universal Lord.

To appreciate this hymn, one needs to remember some key elements of honor cultures. First, although one is rightly entitled to ascribed honor (usually by birth), it is also important not to give the impression that one seeks to augment that honor by impinging on others. Thus, all people learn to practice "cultural humility," that is, staying one step behind one's rightful place. Others clearly see that such a person is no threat to their honor. More than this, others will summon this person to his or her rightful, honorable place.

Though this hymn may appear on a surface reading to reflect the reward of cultural humility, in actuality it does not. The hymn rather points to value reversal: shame leads to honor. In other words, Jesus didn't just politely state his humility, confident that someone would raise him to his proper place. He willingly accepted humiliation in the manner of his death. This is something Jesus' culture would not only not have expected but also would not have encouraged. Thus, any culture like that of our ancestors in the faith who live by honor and shame values would be "shocked" by this message of value-reversal: shame will lead to honor. This hymn presents that notion masterfully. It is likely that with this hymn Paul intended to propose an example for the Philippians to imitate given the situation in which they found themselves.

A second consideration is to keep in mind that Philippi was a Roman colony most of whose citizens were retired from the military. They had strong ties to Rome and would be quite willing to participate in the imperial cult, that is, acknowledging Caesar as divine. It is therefore plausible that Paul is vigorously arguing against such participation. His use of certain words (Lord), proposed gestures (bending the knee), mention of an empire (Phil 2:10), and the acclamation "Jesus is Lord" all echo the language of the imperial cult but speak instead of Jesus. Paul is deliberately commanding the Philippians to acknowledge Jesus as Lord rather than Caesar. This, however, is a treasonous act. What course of action would a retired military person who is devoted to Rome but believes in Jesus choose?

Finally, the downward-upward movement of Jesus' life (humiliation/ exaltation; Phil 2:6-8, 9-11) is reflected in Paul's life. He voluntarily abandons all advantages (Phil 3:4-8) in obedience to God. Then, as slave of God (Phil 1:1), Paul carries this obedience (Phil 1:16) to the point that he might—like Jesus—die a shameful death (Phil 1:20) confident that his glory is to come (Phil 3:10-11). The pattern resonates in the lives of Timothy and Epaphroditus as well. The three live in unselfish obedience and service and are a foil to the self-seeking and selfishness that have crept into the Philippian church.

Of course, today's gospel (Luke 22:14–23:56), the Passion of Jesus, presents in significantly more detail the shameful end of Jesus' life which God reversed a short while later. It also reflects the choice Jesus made between acknowledging his identity and relationship to God and capitulating to his interrogators. Value reversal is a sobering meditation for people in any culture. So too is loyalty. Holy Week provides yet another opportunity to reflect on the death of Jesus and the challenge it poses to all believers.

Easter Sunday–Easter Vigil
Romans 6:3-11

[See John J. Pilch, *The Triduum and Easter Sunday: Breaking Open the Scriptures* (Collegeville: The Liturgical Press, 2000).]

In Romans 5–8 Paul highlights God's love and exhorts the believers living in Rome to "consider yourselves dead to sin and alive to God in Christ Jesus" (6:11). Sin in the singular is noteworthy. Paul is not talking about some sort of human failing. Rather, his Greek word for sin is more correctly understood as a force or a power that drives a person toward an almost unavoidable proneness to failure or to committing an evil deed. Remember that Mediterranean culture views human beings as subject to nature rather than as controlling nature. Nature, in the Mediterranean world, includes an invisible world of powers and forces which mischievously, capriciously, or sometimes even with deliberate calculation intervene in human life and cause human beings to behave in ways that displease God. This world of power and forces is the context in which Paul understands sin.

The good news in Paul's passage is that Jesus' death and resurrection have destroyed the effectiveness of this force or power called sin. Furthermore, baptism snatches believers from the power of this force and incorporates them into new life with God. This is something very real and very welcome in the Mediterranean way of thinking. While some people in this world use amulets, gestures, or incantations to ward off evil, believers through baptism are intimately united with the very one who has defeated the source of all evil.

But people still fail and still commit sins. It is to this situation that Paul speaks when he exhorts his letter-recipients thus: thanks to baptism our old self was crucified (v. 6) and we are now "alive to God in Christ Jesus" (v. 11), therefore, we should live accordingly.

Easter Sunday
Colossians 3:1-4 or 1 Corinthians 5:6b-8

[For introductory comments about Colossians see Fifteenth Sunday in Ordinary Time.]

Colossians 3:1-4. Written by a creative admirer of Paul perhaps between A.D. 63 and 90, this letter presents Jesus as the cosmic Messiah and explains what it means for believers to be exclusively devoted to his service. The letter is addressed to believers living in Colossae, a town in southwestern Turkey near Laodicea not far from modern Pammukale. Today's verses begin the paraenetic, that is, hortatory section of the letters. The message is simple. Since believers through baptism have been raised with Jesus, they ought to focus on matters pertaining to alternate reality (what is above) rather than getting bogged down in material reality (the world in which we live). Today's gospel has some consequences for the ordinary life of the believer: this selection from Colossians puts those consequences in focus.

1 Corinthians 5:6b-8. This most appropriate reading for the feast of the Resurrection is drawn from the letter written around 54 A.D. in which Paul deals more extensively with the physical, human body than in any other letter. For the most part, Paul is concerned with orifices. Our ancestors in the faith realized that orifices were weak points on the body through which it could be penetrated and therefore polluted. In 1 Corinthians 5–7 he focuses on the genitals, a major bodily orifice. The fuller context of today's reading (vv. 1-8) is an incestuous marriage or concubinage between a man and his stepmother. Today's verses have been carved away from this larger segment.

Paul draws an analogy between the effect of yeast and the social consequences of this incestuous union ("not found even among pagans!"). The ancients did not fully understand the fermentation process stimulated by yeast in dough and in saccharine liquids, but they knew how to make practical use of yeast in leavening bread and brewing beer. In Paul's view, the incestuous relationship is a pollutant that threatens the social body, that is, the community of believers, and the marriage partner.

In today's verses, Paul presents the rationale for his thinking. Christ the Paschal Lamb has ended the time of leaven, "the old yeast, the yeast of malice and wickedness." Therefore, it is time to get rid of that old yeast as Israelites did at Passover time. Christians are called to be a new lump of dough, yeast-free, "unleavened bread of sincerity and truth." They must strive to maintain the unity of the social body of the Church. This, of course, is the point of the feast we celebrate today, the resurrection of Jesus, which has important behavioral consequences for the community and all its individual members.

Second Sunday of Easter
Revelation 1:9-11a, 12-13, 17-19

The book of Revelation is the record of John's experiences in altered states of consciousness. He is an astral seer who professes faith in the resurrected Jesus, but he also maintains that he belongs to the house of Israel. The visions took place over an extended period of time. Some preceded the destruction of Jerusalem in A.D. 70, while others were experienced after this date. Obviously, the final edition of this book was sometime after A.D. 70. The basic format of the book is a letter (1:4–3:22; 20:11–22:21) into which various visions have been inserted (4:1–11:19; 12:1–16:21; 17:1–20:10; 21:1–22:5). In vision, John experienced the cosmic Son of Man who gave edicts to the angels of seven Asian Jesus-groups while he was on the island of Patmos, off the coast of Ephesus (Western Turkey).

Today's verses are selected from Part I of the body of the letter to seven Asian churches. The author, John, addresses his fellow Jesus-group prophets ("fellow slaves," 6:11, that is, "[Jesus'] slaves the prophets," 10:7). Together they share distress because they are remaining loyal to Jesus. Who is responsible for the distress? Eventually we shall find out.

The phrase "in spirit" (v. 10, correctly translated in lower case and without the definite article) means "in trance" or in an altered state of consciousness. Ninety percent of people on the face of our planet today have such experiences normally and routinely. The percentage in antiquity was the same or higher. This is one of several ways in which people received direct information from God. The most common was dreams (as Joseph in Matthew 2) or visions (1 Sam 3:1), but other sources included celestial events that impacted on the land below (interpreting stars, comets, lightning, thunder, earthquake, and similar events).

The event mentioned in today's verses took place on the Lord's day, which elevates the value and certainty of John's prophecy. The worst difficulty occurs on the Sabbath (and in the winter), according to Matt 24:20. For first-century Mediterranean peoples, days, months, seasons, and years were controlled by sky forces (see Gal 4:10).

The voice John hears gets his attention and gives him orders. He is to write down what he sees. This will be the divinely revealed letters to seven Asian churches, three on the coast and four inland. The seven golden lampstands reflect the planets, just as the menorah was an ancient symbol of the planetary sky. In the midst of this sky, John sees a constellation which he fleshes out with human form (v. 13: "like a son of man"). John interprets his vision according to the way he learned how to perceive the sky, namely, through Israelite lenses provided by Daniel 7. Ezekiel, Zechariah, and Daniel were still other astral prophets in the Israelite tradition that instructed a person concerning what one might see in the sky.

The constellational being sheds his celestial features and takes on human dimensions, with human-sized hands and feet. Thus, this is a second mode of revelation to John, namely, direct interaction with a celestial being. The being is none other than the risen Jesus, pre-eminent in every respect (First and Last), the Living One alive forever. He has authority over Death and Hades (the abode of the dead). Hades is the personification of the Abyss in the sky at the southern edge of the orb of the earth. This self-identification serves to authorize the being's command to "write down what was, is, and will be." The ancients and modern persons who experience trances come prepared with writing materials.

Today's gospel (John 20:19-31) recounts the disciples' experience of the risen Jesus in an altered state of consciousness.

Such group trance experiences are also common in antiquity and in the modern world. Both of these readings and this season recall for modern believers dimensions of human experience that were lost or deliberately forgotten after the Enlightenment. Thanks to the writing of the Johannine community, we have sources to read, study, and attempt to emulate.

Third Sunday of Easter
Revelation 5:11-14

These verses are drawn from the first insert (Revelation 4–11) into the body of the letter to the Asian churches (1:9–3:22; 20:11–22:25). It explains how God controls the universe and how God dealt with Israel. John went into a trance ("I was in spirit," Rev 4:2) and took a journey to the sky while his feet stayed planted firmly on the ground (4:1). The "open door" is the passageway through which a human being from material reality can enter into alternate reality. Here John sees the throne of God whose right hand is holding a scroll. The scroll contains God's will for Israel (the contents of scrolls was summarized on the outside where all could read it). Opening a scroll put its contents into effect. Who has the sufficient honorable status to open the scroll? The Cosmic Lamb (Aries) standing (therefore alive) as if dead (its head twisted around in such a position that indicates it is dead). This Cosmic Lamb, God's very first creation, was interpreted to be Jesus by the Jesus-group gathered around John.

Today's verses report the huge entourage that surrounds God proclaiming that this Lamb indeed possesses the proper ascribed status to open the seal. The attributes listed are seven in number, indicating total honor. There could be no candidate more honorable than this. The cosmic harmony continues: every creature in heaven, on earth, under the sea and in it–everything in the universe–declares the total honor of God and the Lamb. This in turn is ratified (v. 14) by the

constellational living beings and decan elders. The constellational living beings were introduced in Rev 4:6: four living
creatures full of eyes, that is, stars, hence constellations. The
four constellations are Scorpio-man, Leo, Taurus, and Pega-
sus, each of which has a "royal" star, hence status high enough
to recognize the Lamb's status. The twenty-four elders who
encircle God (Rev 4:4) are celestial personages of exalted
rank (golden crowns, 4:4) and power (enthroned, 4:4). They
are privy to God's cosmic plan and can impart these secrets
to prophets (Rev 5:5; 7:13). In the Israelite tradition (henothe-
istic context), these decans are guardians and rescuers of the
entire cosmos, second only to the highest God (gods) in
power and might. John therefore sees the Celestial Lamb
proclaimed as the champion of God's will.

In today's gospel (John 21:1-19), the risen Jesus appears to
his disciples at the Sea of Tiberias and gives Simon Peter a
new commission, a new direction in life. The experience
takes place in an altered state of consciousness. Today's
verses from Revelation describes its author's altered state of
consciousness in which he meets key personages that will reveal further insights to him. Modern believers know that
human beings actually use less than the full human potential
available to them. Today's readings remind us of one aspect
of the pan-human potential that served our ancestors in the
faith superbly well as they struggled to understand and interpret their experiences. Would that we could activate those
potentials in ourselves.

Fourth Sunday of Easter
Revelation 7:9, 14b-17

In the course of the first insert (Revelation 4–11) into the body of the letter to the Asian churches, the author presents an aside concerning the fate of Israelites who acknowledge the Lamb. This too is part of the author's trance experience. The multitude he sees are Israelites from their own land as well as exiles, colonists, and emigres of earlier generations. This is even larger than the 144,000 from the tribes! The white robes they are wearing mark them as celestial personages. White robes are sky garments. Angels are generally clad in them (Matt 28:3; Mark 16:5). White garments are pure, not soiled, hence they reflect righteousness (Rev 3:18). And since the whiteness of their clothing comes from God, this means God has acknowledged their virtuous behavior and their achievement. God has rewarded their extraordinary loyalty and righteousness. Because of these white garments, these Israelites in the sky are rightly associated with the angels, elders, faithful witnesses before God and the Lamb.

How did these Israelites get here? They survived the time of great distress, they persevered through persecution and became stars or star-like (see Dan 12:3; 4 Esdr 7:97; 4 Macc 17:4-5). John in his trance journey very likely sees them in the Milky Way, which in ancient traditions is where good persons end up and where other writers located them (e.g., Cicero, *The Republic* VI, xvi, 16 and xxvi, 29, the famous passage known as the "Dream of Scipio").

In today's gospel (John 10:27-30), Jesus says of his followers: "I give them eternal life, and they shall never perish." The reading from Revelation offers one understanding that Jesus' listeners would give to "eternal life." How does it compare with images modern believers have of eternal life?

Fifth Sunday of Easter
Revelation 21:1-5a

With these verses we reach the fourth insert (Rev 21:1–22:5) into the body of the letter to the seven Asian churches. The entire text-segment offers four sights in which John describes what is soon to fill the cosmic void. First, John describes the renovated world in general (vv. 1-2) and a descending new Jerusalem. Next, he takes a "virtual" tour of the new Jerusalem (vv. 9-12), with a closer look at the Temple and Throne of God and of the Lamb in that city (21:22–22:5).

In this trance experience, John sees a transformed cosmos, a familiar and traditional theme among Israel's recent prophets (e.g., 1 Enoch 91:16). The reason he could see this already now (in his present) is because in the Israelite understanding, all these realities are already with God having been created by the end of creation week (Genesis 1). The reason why the earth has no sea is that the sea and the entities that control it inevitably produce chaos. The transformed cosmos has no chaos or even the possibility of chaos, so it can't have a sea.

The new center of this cosmos is a genuine "holy city," a new Jerusalem. In antiquity, Mediterranean cities were depicted as women, hence the feminine imagery. Mention of the bride is our first clue as to the identity of the celestial bride whom the cosmic Lamb will marry (see Rev 19:7ff.). Next the majordomo at God's throne announces the new Jerusalem as the place where God will "tent" with his people (recalling Exod 22:7; 40:3 and Israel's Mosaic wilderness sanctuary). Previously God dwelt among Israelites (Exod 25:8; Ps 132:14), but the final sanctuary marks the permanent presence of God (Ezek 37:26-28). In the new cosmos and the new Jerusalem, anything thwarting human well being, from death to pain, will cease to exist. This statement gives moral encouragement to John's community.

In today's gospel (John 13:31-33a, 34-45), Jesus urges his disciples to love one another as he has loved them. The reflections in 1 John indicate how difficult this was for the Johannine community especially when the Secessionists stirred things up (see Sundays after Easter, Year B). Today's verses from Revelation indicate the pay-off for perseverance. Eventually the transformed cosmos will be rid of all chaos. While this is a fond hope eagerly awaited, modern believers would like to "do something" to make it happen sooner. What might that be?

Sixth Sunday of Easter
Revelation 21:10-14, 22-23

In this third (and part of the fourth) sight, John takes a journey (v. 10) to some high mountain to see the final city of humankind. Because of the gargantuan size of the descending new Jerusalem, John in his altered state of consciousness needs to be placed on a great and high mountain. Sky travelers knew two well-attested places for observing the sky, great and high mountains called The Twins, located at the western and eastern ends of the earth. They are attested in the Mesopotamian, Phoenician, Israelite, and Greek traditions. These mountains mark the place of the setting and rising of the sun and other celestial bodies. But this is no ordinary celestial city. It is a bride, the spouse of the Lamb (19:7-9). And its descent marks the wedding of the Lamb.

The city's very structure reveals God's honorable status. It is related to the twelve tribes of the sons of Israel whose names are on the gates (v. 12; see Ezek 48:30-34) and to the Twelve Apostles of the Lamb (foundation names).

The fourth sight mentions something the seer did not see: there was no temple! This is a shock, since all ancient cities had a temple where a visiting deity could reside. Instead, he sees that in the celestial Jerusalem, God is the City's Temple, and he also sees the Lamb. Further, God's honor is ample light supply, and the Lamb is its lamp. The light is adequate for the entire earth (as one might expect from Isa 60:19-20). If there is continuing light, there is abiding security. No need to lock the gates (v. 25) because there is no night!

In today's gospel (John 14:23-29), Jesus promises to send a paraclete who will teach his disciples everything and remind them of what Jesus taught them. In Revelation, John attains new insights through his altered states of consciousness experiences. Relative to the gospel, John the seer views the dwelling of God and the Lamb. Where does God dwell? Where will we live with God and the Lamb?

The Ascension of the Lord
Ephesians 1:17-23 or
Hebrews 9:24-28; 10:19-23

Ephesians 1:17-23. This letter was written by a disciple of Paul probably between 80–100 A.D. These verses are an intercessory prayer on behalf of the letter recipients. The chief hope of the letter writer is that believers grow in knowledge of God, God's activity, and God's gifts. God raised Jesus from the dead and gave him a place of honor next to God in the sky. This makes Jesus a co-regent or ruler with God. In Jesus' risen position he is exalted over angelic and cosmic forces which have such serious impact on the lives of ordinary human beings. Principalities, authorities, powers, and dominions are celestial personages, astral beings who are now subject to Christ. Further, Jesus is head over the Church which is his body. In this letter however, Paul's basic idea is further developed by the one who wrote in his name. Now the Church, Christ's body, benefits from God's all-embracing plan. One of the benefits is to share in the dominion which the head, Jesus, has. Today's gospel (Luke 24:46-53) tells how at his return to the Father, Jesus promises that the Father will clothe his disciples with power from on high. The disciples were filled with great joy.

Hebrews 9:24-28; 10:19-23. Written in the name of Paul sometime between 60–100 A.D., this anonymous author offers a theological reflection about Paul. In these verses, the sacred author returns to the imagery of Yom Kippur, the Day of Atonement (see Leviticus 16), as a type of the death of Jesus (Heb 9:24-28). On this day, the High Priest sacrificed a bull for his own sins and those of the people. Then he entered the Holy of Holies to incense the "mercy seat," the place from which God dispensed mercy to his people, and to sprinkle it with blood from the bull. Next he slaughtered a goat for the sins of the people and sprinkled some of that on the mercy seat, too. The sacred author contrasts this with the sacrifice of Jesus: he died just once which allowed him entry to the presence of God (which is what the mercy seat symbolized) in heaven. The blood of this sacrifice is not that of animals but of Jesus' sacrifice of his life. The effect is Jesus took away sin, once and for all. At his second appearance he will bring salvation which has already been initiated to its final consummation.

Jumping ahead (Heb 10:19-23), the architects of the lectionary focus on the sacred author's two exhortations: to advance (v. 22) and to hold fast to the confession (v. 23). Believers now have fresh access to God because they have a sincere heart that has been sprinkled clean of sin which alludes to baptism, the vehicle by which believers appropriate the effects of Jesus' death and exaltation. The final exhortation is to hold unwaveringly to the promises made by God who can certainly be trusted. Some of the promises have already been fulfilled, while others are still to be attained. But God will not withdraw them, so believers should not waver. These reflections supplement the gospel (Luke 24:46-53), which reports how Jesus ascended to his rightful place at the right hand of the Father. They spell out in more detail what Jesus accomplished and continues to do for believers.

Seventh Sunday of Easter
Revelation 22:12-14, 16-17, 20

The verses of this chapter conclude Revelation as a book (v. 21 concludes the letter, formally). It seems that the compiler of John's visions was interested in collecting whatever observations John the prophet may have made. This is one consideration that helps explain the curious mixture this chapter is. On the other hand, trance experiences are not logical, sequential, with continuity of story. This is because continuity of consciousness is an illusion. Revelation presents reports of sightings from various perspectives. Anyone who has ever had a trance experience recognizes this immediately.

The repetition of "I am coming soon" in vv. 12 and 20 signals an inclusio or inclusion, that is, the author's intention that this section be considered a unity. The cultural information necessary for understanding the first part of the statement of the one coming soon is "balanced reciprocity." Before modern economics came into existence with Karl Marx and Adam Smith, people made a go of it by means of reciprocity. "Balanced reciprocity" means "I do you a favor, now you owe me. You repay me the favor, now I owe you." This goes on and on until one partner can no longer meet the need of the other. So to receive a recompense according to one's deeds is balanced reciprocity. You did this to/for me? I do this to/for you!

The second part of the statement giving one of God's titles previously appeared in Rev 1:8 and 21:6. Here, the emphasis is on the Omega, the last and end quality of what is going on. These letters of the Greek alphabet had cosmic significance. They reveal who God really is, and a person who knows that name is intimate with God. This was a common conviction in the ancient Mediterranean. Plato reports an Orphic saying (*Laws* IV 716A): "However God [as the ancient utterance has it] is the beginning and end and the middle of everything that is."

Verse 16 repeats what was said at the very beginning of this book. The revelation comes from Jesus through his sky servant (1:1-2). And the title "root and offspring of David" also appeared earlier (Rev 5:5). The new title here is "the bright morning star" (see 2 Pet 1:19). To call Jesus by this title is to link him with the planet Aphrodite/Venus. Among all the stars, only Venus casts a shadow by its presence. How can Jesus be compared to a female? Venus as morning star would be male, and as evening star, female. More significant is the function of this star: "light bringer." The Morning Star ushers in the light; Messiah Jesus ushers in the Lord God. The water of life mentioned in v. 1 is now followed in v. 17 with an invitation to come and receive it. The final assurance (v. 20) from Jesus is answered by the community with an affirmation: "Amen! Come Lord Jesus."

In today's gospel (John 17:20-26), Jesus says he "made known [to his disciples] your [God's] name, and I will make it known." Was it the Alpha and Omega title? Or some other? By what name do modern believers call on God?

The Vigil of Pentecost
Romans 8:22-27

According to Paul, three things persuade us of the greatness of the glory or intimate share in God's life which is the destiny of each believer: the testimony of creation (vv. 19-22), the conviction of believers (vv. 23-25), and the testimony of the Spirit (vv. 26-30). Because of Adam's sin (Gen 3:15-17), material nature was cursed, subject to decay itself just like the human beings for whom it had been created. This solidarity in punishment also entails solidarity in redemption. So creation eagerly awaits and groans in labor pains until that final state of glory will be definitively restored. This reflection has special cultural significance. In general, Mediterranean cultures of antiquity recognized that they had absolutely no control over material creation. They were subject to it; they had to suffer and endure it. Thus our ancestors in the faith believed that because of Adam's sin, human beings had no control over nature, yet the redemption of Adam would include the redemption of material creation as well.

What is the basis for Paul's confidence? He draws insight from the notion of first fruits of a harvest (vv. 23-25). When offered to God, these first fruits consecrated the entire harvest and became, as it were, down-payment, pledge, or guarantee of what was still to come. The Spirit serves this purpose for believers (vv. 26-30). Since the believer is already son of God (Rom 8:15), the full implementation of this will include the redemption of the body.

In saying that "we do not know how to pray as we ought" (v. 26), Paul seems to contradict what he said just a few verses earlier, that the Spirit prompts us to pray with confidence: "Abba, my father" (Rom 8:15). It is possible that Paul offers a corrective here to enthusiasm, namely, an exaggerated emphasis on the gifts of the Spirit. It is always possible to be overconfident. The truth is, of course, that because of natural human shortcomings, the Spirit adds its intercessions to our inadequate expressions. God knows this. In today's gospel (John 7:37-39), John illuminates Jesus' statement as a reference to the Spirit which believers would receive. Paul in his turn explains what that Spirit does for believers.

Pentecost
1 Corinthians 12:3b-7, 12-13 or
Romans 8:8-17

1 Corinthians 12:3b-7, 12-13. This letter was probably written about the year 54 A.D. Even a cursory reading of these verses indicates that Paul is insisting on unity. The Corinthian community was so torn by competing party loyalties and dissension that Paul repeatedly exhorts to unity at every opportunity in this letter. The "spirit-people" in Corinth were viewed as the cause of disunity, in part because they were vaunting the Spirit, themselves, and their gifts from the Spirit above others who did not possess such gifts.

It is very difficult for Western individualists to appreciate the harm done by competition in a culture whose core value is honor. By birth, all people in such a culture have ascribed honor. It is shameful and wrong to attempt to improve that status. The cultural obligation is to maintain and preserve it. Cooperation, harmony, and unity are the preferred and honorable values in a collectivistic society.

The combination of select verses for today's reading highlight two powerful arguments that Paul mounts against such divisive competition. One argument is based on how three heavenly figures relate to each other. After admitting that the Spirit does indeed grant various gifts, forms of service, and workings, Paul notes–in an apparent hierarchic ordering–that the Spirit, the Lord, and God live in harmony and not in rivalry or competition. God, of course, is sovereign and holds the highest place on the honor map (see 1 Cor 11:3; 15:27-28). And the authentic Spirit acknowledges that Jesus has a special position: "Jesus is Lord." Thus, after God, Jesus enjoys the next maximum status, and the Spirit holds third place as servant of the Lord Jesus. The three are not equal in role or status, yet they live harmoniously in heaven. The Spirit and the Spirit's gifts, therefore, should not disrupt the order God has for the world. The second argument is based on the human body which consists of different parts, all of which must work together harmoniously lest damage occur to the body.

This exaggerated sense of self-esteem and exalted status among the "spirit people" amounts to a denial of authority. Their understanding of the freedom bestowed upon them by the Spirit calls into question God's will for specific patterns of roles, statuses, and orderly relationships on earth and in heaven. Paul argues that the pattern existing in heaven ought to be mirrored on earth. In the concluding verses (12-13), Paul declares that not only is the diversity of gifts among human beings unified in the same Spirit, but the diversity of races (Israelites and non-Israelites) and roles (slaves or free persons) is similarly unified in the "one" Spirit.

Romans 8:8-17. Paul wrote this letter around 57–58 A.D. from Corinth or Cenchrae, its port. Today we encounter another set of contrasting words that Paul likes to use in discussing the human condition: flesh and spirit. Flesh connotes natural, concretely material human existence. In these verses it is equivalent to slavery and suggests something outside of God's realm. Paul connects flesh with Death: "the concern of the flesh is death" (Rom 8:6). Moreover, "the concern of the flesh is hostility toward God; it does not submit to the law of God, nor can it; and those who are in the flesh cannot please God" (Rom 8:7-8). It is a rather depressing picture. In contrast, spirit denotes freedom and suggests things of God and heaven. It is the very power which raised Jesus' human and mortal body from death to holiness and life (Rom 8:10).

In the Israelite tradition, human beings were pulled in two different directions or ways by different spirits: good ones and evil ones. Human beings are caught in the middle of a battle that never ends: in the heavens, on earth, and within the individual person. The question is: which spirit will "lord" it over a person? The same is true of the on-going struggle between flesh and spirit. "For the flesh has desires against the Spirit, and the Spirit against the flesh" (Gal 5:17). Romans 8:1-17, which describes the working's of God's Spirit unto salvation, balances the preceding section (Rom 7:7-12) in which Paul describes himself at the mercy of a force that is not of God. From this perspective, the reader can sense and appreciate Paul's relief and the urgency with which he exhorts the letter recipients to live by the Spirit. It is this Spirit which makes believers children of God who can confidently call him "Abba, Father!"

The gospel (John 20:19-23 or John 14:15-16, 23b-26) describes yet other gifts of the Spirit (power to forgive and retain sins; guidance to all truth) intended to maintain unity in the community.

Trinity Sunday
Romans 5:1-5

A new emphasis emerges in chapter five (previously Paul spoke of the utter hopelessness of human existence without Jesus Messiah: 1:18–3:20; then salvation through faith in Jesus Messiah: 3:21–4:25). Paul reflects on the life of a person who has accepted Jesus as Messiah. In chapter five justification and righteousness recede from major consideration, while God's love comes to the fore. In today's select verses, Paul considers how it feels to be right with God.

The two principal effects of being in right relationship with God are peace (v. 1) and hope (v. 2). The peace Paul speaks of is that calm and relief which human beings experience after wrestling with and resolving great doubts or problems. In the anti-introspective culture of the Middle East, doubts and other such problems tend to be somatized. When they are resolved, the results bring peace and restore wholesomeness and physical health.

In vv. 3-4 Paul employs a literary device, sorites, that presents a chain-like string of ideas which a listener would find difficult to challenge or disagree with. The word "knowing," which initiates the series, presumes everyone agrees with what will follow. It is true that the Israelite (see Deut 8:2-5; Prov 3:11-12; etc.) and the Stoic traditions believed that suffering could be disciplinary and could strengthen character. But experience also indicated that people who suffer can sink into despair and bitterness. For Paul, the key to hope is

Jesus. As his sufferings led to his honor, so hopefully will that happen in the lives of those united with him.

Hope or trust is confidence to such a degree that one puts everything into the hands of the trusted person. Here, the object of such hope or trust is the confidence of sharing in God's honor. Paul boasts about this hope. In the Bible, boasting is the way in which one acknowledges one's personal lord and master, in this case, God. If through sin a person has shamed God and become thereby a shameful person, what a remarkable reversal of life-situation to now share in the immeasurable honor and glory of God. This is truly an amazing gift from God. Indeed, Paul goes on to explain this in vv. 5-8. That Jesus, who didn't deserve to die this death, agreed to die for sinners is an incredible thought. In a cultural world which operates predominantly by informal exchanges known as dyadic contract (I do you a favor, you owe me. You repay the favor, I owe you; etc.), that Jesus would do us a favor which is truly impossible for us to repay is truly astounding. Yet, that is indeed how God proves his love for us. God's ways are not the ways of human beings.

In the gospel (John 16:12-15) Jesus admits that some of what his disciples must still learn they "cannot bear now." Perhaps modern believers feel this way when they read Romans. It is a challenging epistle, just as challenging as it is to grasp the mystery of the Trinity. Is it necessary to understand everything perfectly in order to love God?

Eleventh Sunday
in Ordinary Time
Galatians 2:16, 19-21

[For background, see Ninth Sunday in Ordinary Time, above, where this semi-continuous reading of Galatians began.] In these verses, Paul sums up the first two chapters of this letter and introduces the next two. Believers are made right with God by being loyal to the deity (by faith) and not by means of legal observances ("works of the law"). Western readers who hear the word "law" think of laws familiar in the culture, or if they are believers they may think of Church or "canon" law. While translators put the English word "law" on Paul's lips, it is imperative to keep in mind that he was speaking of *torah*, a Hebrew word that essentially means instruction or directive. The first five books of the Hebrew Bible are called "Torah" because in them God gives instructions and directives that help a person achieve the core values of the chosen people, namely, *shalom* or peace. *Shalom* is a dynamic state in which a person continues to achieve complete identity as a limited, finite, free human being.

Paul of course wrote his letters in Greek. The Greek word he used for *torah* is the same one the Septuagint translators used: *nomos*. While modern translators usually render this Greek word into English as "law," all dictionaries list a broader range of meanings. Yet as should always be the case, it is the historical and cultural context that helps determine the appropriate meaning of a word. In the period of the Israelite monarchy (or the restoration after the Babylonian exile), *torah* (or *nomos* in the Septuagint version of documents from these historical periods) can appropriately be translated "law." In its strict sense, law is a body of binding rights and obligations that have been twice institutionalized–once in custom, then again in the legal or political realm. In Israel's time of self-rule, *torah* was law in this strict sense.

But in Paul's day (and prior to this in the Hellenistic period–300 B.C. to A.D. 6), Israel lived under the law of its conquerors. In this setting, *torah* is reduced to custom (that is, rules or norms embedded in society's institutions) legitimated by God. (Rules are explicit instructions or directives; norms are implicit instructions or directives.) The customs were embedded in family or kinship, and politics or government, that is, the basic social institutions of Mediterranean culture.

Thus, in his own lifetime (Roman rule), Paul used to be a Torah-observing Pharisee. He studied and lived the Torah as normative Israelite custom legitimated by God. But once he learned that God raised Jesus from the dead, and that Jesus is Messiah, Paul realized that God removed divine approval from normative Israelite customs enshrined in Torah. Moreover, Jesus' resurrection has reshaped human life at its core. Jesus as Lord has become a life-giving spirit (1 Cor 15:45) that directs human behavior.

The gospel (Luke 7:36–8:3) contrasts a Pharisee with Jesus in their different attitudes toward a sinner. The Pharisee, very much like Paul before his change of outlook, continues to use *torah*, normative Israelite customs presumed legitimated by God, to judge the woman. Jesus, through whom God offers forgiveness to the woman (notice the "theological" passive voice in vv. 47-48) understands God differently, takes a different view of the woman, and offers a model for his followers to emulate.

Twelfth Sunday in Ordinary Time
Galatians 3:26-29

Through faith, believers are (literally) sons of God. Inclusive language translations (such as the Revised NAB) render the phrase "children of God" for the sake of modern Western contexts and sensitivities. Paul's preceding discussion (vv. 23-25) comparing the Torah to a pedagogue derives from the system of education in his day which was predominantly intended for young boys. The pedagogue accompanied the boy from the home to the school. This broader context helps to understand and interpret Gal 3:28, which is widely used in modern discussion to proclaim sweeping egalitarianism that is difficult to imagine in circum-Mediterranean culture.

"You are all one in Christ Jesus" (Gal 3:28 Revised NAB) links with the previous sentiment: "For through faith you are all children [literally, sons] of God in Christ Jesus" (Gal 3:26, Revised NAB). Paul's intent is to personalize his remarks and stir up once again the emotional anchorage these letter recipients once had to the gospel Paul preached but which they abandoned (Gal 1:6-9). What counts above all is union with and adherence to Jesus. Secondary differences (ethnicity, gender, social status) can and should be kept in proper secondary perspective. Paul appears to be advising in these verses the same thing he says in 1 Cor 7:17-28: don't be distracted by secondary differences. As Pauline scholar Joseph

Fitzmyer observes: "Such unity in Christ does not imply political equality in church or society" (*New Jerome Biblical Commentary* 47:25).

In today's gospel (Luke 9:18-24), Jesus demonstrates the Middle Eastern cultural humility so typical of collectivistic persons: each learns his/her identity from the group and strives to live up to it. Paul spells it out: we are all one in Christ Jesus; members of this community have a clear model to emulate.

Thirteenth Sunday in Ordinary Time
Galatians 5:1, 13-18

Finally, Paul draws practical conclusions from the preceding four chapters of his letter. He urges those who have slipped in their resolve or who have backslided in their status to dig in, to stand firm, to yield not another inch to anyone. At issue is a return to circumcision which Paul opposed and rejected as a requirement for non-Israelites to become followers of Jesus.

Once again tugging at the letter recipients' emotions ("brothers and sisters," v. 13), Paul presents another understanding of "freedom." He discourages using freedom for unfettered self-indulgence. "Serve one another through love" (v. 13). Literally, the Greek verb translated here as "serve one another" should be "render slave service" to one another. The Israelite understanding which Paul reflects is that no human person is ever absolutely free, subject to no one. The Exodus freed the Israelites from Egyptian bondage so that they might serve (render slave service to) God more faithfully. By raising Jesus from the dead, God gave an opportunity for those who believe in Jesus to attain a new freedom, a freedom for a new kind of slave service. For those united in Jesus, secondary differences are not important (gender, social status, ethnicity). What really counts is "faith working through love" (Gal 5:6).

To make his instruction concrete, Paul draws on two favorite images: flesh and spirit. Flesh refers to the human person as entirely self- reliant, weak, earthbound, unredeemed. Spirit refers to the knowing and willing core of the individual, that part of a human person most suitable for receiving and responding to God's Spirit. Paul's advice: walk according to the prompting of the Spirit.

In the gospel (Luke 9:51-62), to put it in Paul's terms, Jesus rebukes his disciples and the petitioners for wanting to gratify the desire of the flesh: punish the Samaritans (follow Jesus for sake of adventure, allow filial piety to deter from following Jesus) and urges them instead to listen to the guidance of God's spirit.

Fourteenth Sunday
in Ordinary Time
Galatians 6:14-18

Beginning with Gal 6:11, Paul adds a "postscript" to the letter in his own handwriting. The previous part was dictated to a scribe. In a society whose core cultural value is honor, boasting plays a very important role. In the Galatian communities, Paul's opponents have sought to shame Paul by denying he is an apostle, claiming his gospel is incomplete, and urging those originally loyal to Paul to switch their loyalties to them. Their successes are their boast. Paul's response is that he has died to all this jockeying for honor because the death and resurrection of Jesus into which believers are baptized offers the possibility of a dramatically new way of living. In this perspective whether one is circumcised or not is absolutely meaningless. What counts more than anything is to be reshaped at the core of one's existence by immersion in the paschal mystery. Those who have embraced Jesus as Messiah and shared in God's salvific plan are the true Israel of God standing in contrast to the "Israel according to the flesh" (1 Cor 10:18).

One can almost sense Paul's exhausted exasperation in his concluding comment. "From now on, let no one make troubles for me." The Greek word for the "marks" of Jesus which Paul claims to carry is "stigmata." That word did not mean in antiquity what it means today. Paul's intention here is to contrast circumcision, the "mark" in which his opponents gloried, with the wounds of Jesus in which Paul shares by having made Jesus' rite of passage from death to life. Visible signs of those wounds resulted from Paul's many sufferings: illness (Gal 4:13), floggings (2 Cor 11:25), and much more for the sake of Christ. These visible signs constitute for him so many "marks" branding him for eternity as "the slave of Messiah Jesus" (Gal 1:10).

It is fitting to recall as today's gospel reminds worshipers (Luke 10:1-12, 17-20) that Jesus sent his disciples on mission "like lambs among wolves" (v. 3). This seems to describe quite accurately Paul's experience with his opponents in Galatia, though clearly Paul was anything but a docile lamb that kept silent when faced with slaughter. Paul reminds the modern believer to wear with pride the scars of risk, the stretch marks of revision, and the scars of wounds gained in battles for convictions rooted in the gospel.

Fifteenth Sunday in Ordinary Time
Colossians 1:15-20

Modern scholars locate this letter among the Deutero-Paulines written between A.D. 70 and 80 by someone who knew the Pauline tradition quite well. Perhaps it is a product of a Pauline school tradition located in Ephesus. Verse 14 speaks of "forgiveness of sins," one of thirty-eight such words or phrases which occur nowhere in the undisputed Pauline writings (see Eph 1:7; Heb 9:22; 10:18), supporting the argument against authenticity as a letter of Paul.

Beginning in v. 15, the sacred author introduces a primitive Christian hymn originating perhaps in the liturgy. Differences in the vocabulary, style, and thought content from the rest of Colossians and from the undisputed Paulines confirms this judgment. It is similar to hymns found in Qumran and to the prologue of John's Gospel (1:1-18). The theme of the hymn is the role of Jesus in creation.

The Hellenistic Judaic tradition claimed that wisdom, which was created first, was also an agent or partner in YHWH's work of creation. Wisdom motifs are echoed throughout this hymn (Wis 7:22; 9:2-4; see also Prov 3:19; 8:22-31). A key idea, however, is that Jesus is the "image" of the invisible God (v. 15). Medieval Franciscan theologians like John Duns Scotus used this hymn to argue the absolute primacy of Christ. In order for the invisible God to create a human being in the divine image and likeness, God needed a model. Jesus incarnate, "the firstborn of all creation," was the model or image. The philosophical axiom that the first thing one thinks of (e.g., a cake) is the last thing to happen (after gathering ingredients, mixing, then baking) fleshed out the argument. God thought of Jesus incarnate first and eventually, in the course of time which doesn't affect God, Jesus was born.

In Jesus all other created beings in the sky and on earth, visible and invisible, whether angelic or astral, came into being. He is indeed the head of the cosmic body, but the sacred author appears to have added "the church" in v. 18, shifting the image to Jesus as head of the Church which is an important theme in Colossians (1:24, 27; 2:17, 19; 3:15). The community as body is certainly present in the authentic Paulines, but Christ as head of the body is a later development. As the hymn concludes, it praises Jesus as preeminent and reconciling all things, thus establishing and solidifying unity in the entire cosmos and in the Church (see feast of Christ the King, Cycle C, below).

Today's gospel (Luke 10:25-37) takes our heads out of the sky and plants our feet firmly on the earth with the familiar story of the man beaten and left half dead at the roadside. Taken by itself, the story is interesting and challenging. When coupled with the cosmic view of today's epistle, the believer grasps the bigger picture of God's plan. How can a modern believer share with needy victims in today's world the benefits of Christ's lordship over the cosmos and over his body, the Church? How can the modern believer be image of Christ for others, as Christ is image of the invisible God?

Sixteenth Sunday in Ordinary Time
Colossians 1:24-28

This is one of two reflections in this letter about Paul as a minister of the gospel. Though written by a disciple of Paul after his death, the sacred author recalls one of Paul's imprisonments (perhaps together with Epaphras, see Col 1:7). Whatever the case, Epaphras has communicated the difficulties that are besetting this faith community. These believers or Messianists of non-Israelite origin are finding esoteric Judaism, which may have incorporated elements from pagan philosophy and Greek mystery religions, a very attractive alternative to what they originally learned.

The sacred author's response is that they, God's holy ones, those non-Israelites who have received the gospel, have also learned the mystery, thanks to God revealing it. The mystery is: "Christ in you," that is, Jesus is now present among such persons in the gospel as it is preached among them. The entire purpose of preaching Jesus to non-Israelites was to present for all persons the possibility of having a right relationship with God. It was Paul's ardent commitment to present every person as "perfect in Christ," in other words, perfect in a unique and distinctive way patterned after the quality and direction of the life of Jesus.

In the mystery religions, knowledge of cosmic or divine secrets was available only to a privileged few, but here as Paul indicates, it is revelation open and available to all—the word of God, Christ in you. In Israelite tradition, the mystery referred to God's plan for history. Only God could make this known. Human beings are incapable of figuring it out on their own. When God called Paul to be an apostle, God revealed the mystery of the gospel and its relevance for non-Israelites.

Finally, what does the sacred author mean by "filling up" with his sufferings "what is lacking in the afflictions of Christ"? Surely nothing was lacking in what Christ suffered. But the Israelite tradition believed that woes and tribulations would have to be endured before the return of the Messiah (see Luke 21:10-11; Mark 13:19-20; etc.). Yet the quota of tribulations set and known by God alone can be shortened for the sake of the elect. Thus Paul by his sufferings as an apostle is hoping to shorten the time before the Messiah's Second Coming. At the same time, it is clear that evangelists and others believed that those who proclaim the gospel would have to endure suffering and hardships. In today's gospel (Luke 10:38-42), Jesus observes that one should not be anxious and worried about many things. There is need of only one. The sacred author of Colossians encourages his letter recipients to be focused on the mystery preached to them; forget about everything else. This is good advice for modern believers too.

Seventeenth Sunday in Ordinary Time
Colossians 2:12-14

These verses are part of the sacred author's response to a certain kind of Judaic mystic group which offered an attractive package of dietary and sexual abstinence coupled with fervent piety that all but guaranteed salvation. The author's argument is two-fold. He reminds the Colossian believers about what the Messiah has accomplished for them through his death and resurrection. In effect, the burdensome and accusatory law has been nailed to the cross.

Colossians 2:12 appears to summarize Rom 6:1-11 concerning the believer's identification with Jesus' death and resurrection in baptism. There is, however, a significant difference. In Romans, believers will be united to the resurrection in the future, while in Colossians, this resurrection has already taken place. In the sacred author's view, faith in the God who raised Jesus was expressed in baptism. As a result, Colossians have shared in Jesus' death and resurrection. The agent is God.

More importantly, believers have been initiated into a far greater mystery than the one claimed by misguided ascetics and visionaries. Baptism, much more effective and powerful than circumcision, bestows new life to a dead body. That is much more significant than ritual-surgical removal of a flap of skin. Also, the human race's IOU to God stipulating penalties for failure to pay has been wiped clear by Jesus' death and resurrection. A new relationship to God is now possible.

Jesus' prayer and reflections on the significance of prayer in today's gospel (Luke 11:1-13) is buttressed by the assurances of the sacred author of Colossians. Believers have a lot going for them with God. They should be courageous and bold.

Eighteenth Sunday in Ordinary Time
Colossians 3:1-5, 9-11

[For Col 3:1-4, see Easter Sunday.] Today's verses begin the paraenetic, that is, hortatory section of the letters. The message is simple. Since believers through baptism have been raised with Jesus, they ought to focus on matters pertaining to alternate reality (what is above) rather than getting bogged down in material reality (the world in which we live). Baptism (not far in the background of these verses) has done three things for believers: you have died with Christ, you have been raised with him, and as a result you will share in his glorious coming. Between now and then, the fullness of risen life and glory remains hidden with Christ in God.

This is the foundation for rejecting the list of "vices" presented in vv. 9-11. The imperative "put to death" flows from baptismal imagery in which the believers identify with Jesus' death. Four of the five vices seem to relate to forbidden sexual activity. The fifth, greed, is linked with idolatry. Actually, in the Israelite tradition, idolatry was generally spoken of in terms of sexual activity, hence this entire list of five likely relates to idolatry, or failure to recognize or acknowledge God. Such behaviors root one too deeply in material reality and made it difficult to seek the things of alternate reality. Indeed, steady pursuit of such a life-style will result in God's judgment and make for a very unhappy place in alternate reality.

The command to "stop lying to one another" does not signal a peculiar shortcoming among the letter-recipients. Secrecy, deception, and lying are acceptable strategies for protecting one's honor and reputation in Mediterranean society. However, since in baptism believers have "taken off" the old self to "put on" a new self, there should be no need for secrecy, deception, and lying, culturally ingrained though it may be. As Jesus himself said: "Let your 'Yes' mean 'Yes,' and your 'No' mean 'No'!" (Matt 5:37).

The concluding verse probably reflects an early Christian baptismal formula similar to Gal 3:28, though the omission of male and female appears to throw the focus on ethnic differences which in Christ disappear as insignificant. Very likely, the full force of this formula is lost on modern readers, especially since male and female—an item of contemporary interest in the West—are not mentioned. Who cares about the rest? Actually, the ancient world cared very much. It tended to stereotype on the basis of these categories. "Judeans have no dealings with Samaritans" (John 4:9). "It is unlawful for a Judean to associate with or visit anyone of another nation" (Acts 10:28). To say as our sacred author does that such distinctions no longer matter is revolutionary indeed. Yet the final formula, "Christ is all in all," which is a natural conclusion from the hymn in Col 1:15-20, justifies the judgment.

The rich man in today's parable (Luke 12:13-21) who refuses to be a patron was condemned by God. The ancients understood this well, though Americans might wonder what is wrong with planning for one's retirement as he did. In the words of today's epistle, his mind was on "what is on earth" rather than on "what is above." Both readings offer much food for thought especially for those who live in secular cultures and plan their lives according to modern economics. The one word that links both readings—even if only superficially—is greed.

Nineteenth Sunday in Ordinary Time
Hebrews 11:1-2, 8-19

Writing in the name of Paul sometime between 60–100 A.D. this anonymous author offers theological reflection about Jesus. The whole of Hebrews 11 is a carefully constructed unit reflecting on faith (see the inclusio or inclusion formed in vv. 1-2 and 39-40 by the notion of receiving witness through faith). It begins with a definition of faith (vv. 1-2) and then reviews biblical heroes who illustrate his notion of faith. Today's verses focus on Sarah the Matriarch and Abraham the Patriarch.

The sacred author understands faith to have two dimensions: it relates to the attainment of hoped-for goals and to the perception of invisible realities. It is the latter that supports a believer in trials and tribulations which test one's faith, or as the Mediterranean world would understand it, one's loyalty. What are some of the invisible realities (things not seen) that motivate a believer to remain faithful and loyal? Of course, God ("the one who is invisible," 11:27), God's existence and providence (11:6), trustworthiness (11:11), and power (11:19).

The story of Abraham as a model of faith is presented in three sections: his election, migration, and reception of the promised child (vv. 8-12); Abraham as a sojourner (vv. 13-16); and the binding of Isaac (vv. 17-22). In the first section (vv. 8-12), the sacred author of Hebrews stretches his sources, as is common in retelling biblical traditions. Verses 10 and 11 attribute motivations to the characters which do not appear in the original account and are implausible in that original context. But for the sacred author, this introduces his reflective comments in the next four verses (vv. 13-16). So faith, sticking with God no matter what, motivates Abraham to obey and to endure while patiently waiting to achieve the promised goal. One ought not press the biological comments in vv. 11 and 12. The real focus is the birth of Isaac, the child of promise. Life can come from death through faith.

The second segment praises the loyalty of the patriarchs who were seeking not an earthly but a heavenly homeland. It interrupts the reflection on Abraham. Clearly this reflection is for the benefit of the sacred author's audience, fellow believers in Jesus. Their faith has caused alienation from family and home and rendered them sojourners, subject to the suffering that accompanies alien status.

The final segment resumes the story of Abraham with his willingness to sacrifice his son who was the foundation of the fulfillment of God's promises. Again the sacred author restates the motif that God can bring life from death.

In today's gospel (Luke 12:32-48), Jesus urges his disciples to seek the "inexhaustible treasure in heaven" which the Father has prepared. The epistolary verses highlight the loyalty (= faith) that is required to keep a steady eye on that goal which will eventually be reached.

Twentieth Sunday in Ordinary Time
Hebrews 12:1-4

As the reflection on faith came to end, the sacred author noted that loyalty is closely associated with enduring persecution. Chapter 12 reinforces that association, drawing upon imagery from athletics, namely, running the race (12:1-13). The introduction (vv. 1-3) summarizes the preceding chapter and introduces the idea of the race. Next (vv. 4-6) the author quotes Proverbs and explains it (vv. 7-11), which provides him with a practical application (vv. 12-13).

The call to endurance is grounded in Jesus who by enduring the cross now sits at the right side of the throne of God. Runners must travel light, hence put off any weight (sin) and persevere in the marathon. Perseverance and endurance are words associated with martyrdom (4 Macc 17:10, 12, 17), so the exhortation is serious and concerns more than a race. Jesus, on whom the runners are to fix their eyes, is the first human to have attained faith's goal, the inheritance of God's promise. He is the "first runner" (leader) and perfecter of unswerving loyalty. Therefore, Jesus' followers ought not to flag in endurance.

Careful readers of this passage will note that Jesus "endured the cross, despising its shame." Once again the sacred author is reinterpreting for his letter recipients. In Jesus' life-setting, it seems that he had no influential friends to help him avoid arrest and trial (see Matt 5:25). While the form of execution (crucifixion) was indeed shameful, reserved for criminals, Jesus endured it in eminently manly fashion, making a strong impression on the pagan centurion who stood guard (Mark 15:39). Trial was no guarantee of justice (see Prov 20:3; 25:8-10, 18), so Jesus made the best of this bad situation in his life. By raising Jesus from the dead, however, God caused Jesus' followers to reconsider the traditional cultural understanding of honor and shame, and the sacred author could then reinterpret Jesus' death as "despising its shame."

In today's gospel (Luke 12:49-53), Jesus recognizes the challenge that loyalty to him will pose to many families, the focal social institution in his culture. The author of Hebrews reminds his readers that they "have not yet resisted to the point of shedding blood." There is a heavy price to pay in following Jesus, but the reward is certainly worth it.

Twenty-First Sunday in Ordinary Time
Hebrews 12:5-7, 11-13

[For related background, see Fifth Sunday of Lent, Year B.] Today's verses explain how suffering is God's way of teaching and disciplining God's children. The sacred author cites Prov 3:11-12 and then interprets and applies it to the life-setting of the letter recipients. To appreciate the sacred author's point, let us review the process by which young boys were raised from infancy to puberty. [Review Twenty-Eighth Sunday in Ordinary Time, Year B.] A wife was not fully integrated into her husband's family until she bore a son (cf. 1 Sam 1:1-19, esp. v. 8). The birth of a son was great joy for all. Boys were raised by all the women with little or no male presence until the age of puberty. They were pampered, pleasured, and in modern terms quite "spoiled." Lacking male role models during this time of life, they entered puberty with a sense of gender-ambiguity. At puberty, without the assistance of a rite of passage (bar mitzvah is Talmudic in origin), boys were pushed unceremoniously into the harsh and hierarchical world of men. They ran back to the comforts of the women's world, but the women would simply return them to the men's world.

Proverbs (e.g., 13:24; 23:13) and Sirach (30:1, 12) prescribe frequent and severe physical discipline of boys as a means of instilling obedience and subordination. The patriarch was effective only if he could impose his will upon and secure the unswerving loyalty of his sons, something the father in Jesus' parable failed to accomplish (Luke 15:11-32). Eventually the adolescent son would become a man and spend his life continuing to learn how and trying to prove it (see the Servant Songs in Isaiah, the model of a cultural hero for males to imitate).

The author of Hebrews argues that good people suffer not because God is punishing them but rather as a sign of affection. He draws this conclusion about God as father from the experience of honorable and good Mediterranean fathers described above. His final exhortation returns to athletic imagery of the race. Drooping hands and weak knees are traditional images of exhaustion (Isa 35:3; Deut 32:36). Reference to "lame" may be the author's insinuation that the community to whom the letter is addressed needs to "shape up."

Inclusive language translations of the passage from Proverbs and this section of Hebrews tend to translate "son" as child/children. Such a rendition does not reflect Mediterranean culture honestly. Boys are physically disciplined; girls are not. While the revised NAB translates "son/s" here, the architects of the lectionary have unfortunately replaced "sons" with "children" in v. 5. This unwittingly provides biblical warrant for modern readers to physically discipline girls as well as boys. In Western culture, physical discipline is usually disapproved as a child rearing strategy, just as the Mediterranean cultural fusion of love and violence in Proverbs 3 repeated in Hebrews is also not an acceptable pattern of interpersonal behavior in the West. It is important to be sensitive to these cultural differences.

In today's gospel (Luke 13:22-30), Jesus urges his disciples to strive to enter "through the narrow gate." Attaining salvation requires effort, the kind of effort demanded in a marathon race. Yet, as the popular saying has it, no gain without the pain.

Twenty-Second Sunday in Ordinary Time
Hebrews 12:18-19, 22-24a

In today's verses, the author offers motivation for his injunction in v. 14: "Strive for peace with everyone, and for that holiness without which no one will see the Lord." He compares current believers with their forebears in the Exodus. At Mount Sinai, they experienced a theophany of God (vv. 18-19). But current believers draw near to a new holy mountain, Zion, which in contrast is not a place of terror but rather one of joyous celebration. Not only are current believers not denied access to God, but they are part of this new assembly in heaven. Jesus has made this possible.

In Hebrews, the word "approach" is used to describe how believers come to a relationship with God (4:16; 7:25; 10:22; 11:6). At Sinai those who heard God speak did not want any other message to be added (compare Exod 20:19; Deut 5:25). The idea is that what was said was sufficient. Then the author of Hebrews presents a series of four paired items to describe the new and superior reality which his letter recipients approach. The pairs are: mountain (Sion)–city (Zion/Jerusalem); countless angels–the assembly of human beings; God the judge–spirits of the departed righteous in God's presence; and mediator–sprinkled blood of the covenant.

In today's gospel (Luke 14:1, 7-14) Jesus tells a parable about people seeking places of honor but concludes by telling behavior more suitable to winning honor at the "resurrection of the righteous." The author of Hebrews describes this very honorable place for the righteous. The contrasts are intended to make the listener ask: Why settle for less?

Twenty-Third Sunday in Ordinary Time
Philemon 9-10, 12-17

Brief though this letter is, it poses huge challenges to understanding and interpretation. On the face of it, the matter looks simple. Onesimus, a slave owned by Philemon, ran away to Paul and through Paul's instruction became a believer in Jesus. Paul writes this letter from prison (most likely in Ephesus, around A.D. 55) and recommends that Philemon, who already was a believer, receive the returning runaway without seeking any retribution.

To begin with, it is important for the modern reader to realize that slavery in antiquity had nothing in common with slavery as it existed in the New World. Important and interesting as this topic is, it is not the chief point of the letter nor should it constitute a major focus of reflection. It suffices to know that owners usually pursued runaway slaves and rewarded those who captured or aided in their capture. In sending Onesimus back to Philemon, Paul complies with Roman law that required the return of runaway slaves.

Of greater interest is the horizon of cultural values that Paul may be attempting to activate on behalf of Onesimus. First, he sports his age: "an old man" (the Greek word ordinarily designates someone between the ages of fifty and sixty). Since Philemon is younger, the entire range of honor-obligations between younger and older men come into play (see, e.g., Sir

32:7-9; 3:12-16). Though he does not explicitly make any claim, it is difficult to deny that by referring to himself as an old man Paul intended to activate appropriate values and behaviors in Philemon.

Further, Paul's use of kinship language in a culture where kinship is the focal social institution is also calculated for effect. Paul has become surrogate father to Onesimus by bringing him to faith in Jesus Messiah. In sending Onesimus back to Philemon, Paul says he is sending "my own heart." The Greek word translated "heart" literally means "viscera" and can serve as a synonym for "child" (Artemidorus, *Dreams,* 1.44: "Children, like the inward parts of the body, are called viscera" [the same Greek word Paul uses: *splangchna*]). Thus it is not affection so much as integral filial relationship that Paul asserts. Philemon, too, was brought to faith by Paul and therefore is also Paul's child. These three are now fictive kin, a surrogate family. Family rules now come into play, and the main thing that keeps a family together is the group-glue which our ancestors in the faith called "love." It was not an emotion or affection so much as loyalty and determination to keep the group whole. Thus Onesimus is now not just a slave but a brother to Philemon "as a man and in the Lord." Notice how the "Christian" motivation is deeply embedded in the complex of cultural values.

In today's concluding statement, "if you regard me as a partner [in faith]," Paul lays his reputation on the line and makes a veiled threat of shaming Philemon (bolstered in the next verses in which Paul promises to pay any of Onesimus' debts to Philemon—this kind of exchange simply does not exist between friends and brothers). If Philemon acts otherwise than Paul is requesting, the entire house church will know it, and his reputation will be ruined among them.

Today's gospel (Luke 14:25-33) highlights the fact that following Jesus may entail abandoning one's family of origin, but one will have a surrogate family of fellow believers. The obligations in the surrogate family may become more demanding than in the family of origin. That, of course, seems to be played out in the scenario with Paul, Philemon, and Onesimus. No one ever said being a Christian was a simple matter.

Twenty-Fourth Sunday in Ordinary Time
1 Timothy 1:12-17

This letter is one of the Pastoral epistles (along with 2 Timothy and Titus). They have been called Pastoral epistles since the eighteenth century because they are addressed to "pastors" of the early community. For this reason, the anonymous person who wrote this letter around A.D. 100 under the name of Paul is usually called "the Pastor." Timothy was appointed to head the church in Ephesus. In 1 Tim 1:3-20, the Pastor addresses a major problem plaguing this community: false teachers. Timothy is exhorted to urge teachers to be orthodox (vv. 3-5). False teachers miss the mark (vv. 6-7), but we good teachers know better (vv. 8-11). Paul's personal example is encouraging and worthy of imitation (vv. 12-17), therefore the charge for Timothy is well within that church leader's ability and competence (vv. 18-20). It was common for teachers to exhort disciples to imitate and share in their striving for perfection.

Today's verses present a harsher picture of Paul's conversion than other reports (see e.g., Gal 1:11-16; Phil 3:4-8; though compare Acts 9:1-19). It is a carefully constructed piece: notice the two statements of praise (vv. 12 and 17) and the repeated phrase "mercifully treated" (vv. 13-16). In other words, this is "ring composition": A–the praise (v. 12); B–mercifully treated (v. 13); C–Jesus came to save sinners; I'm the foremost (vv. 14-15); B'–mercifully treated (v. 16); A'– the praise (v. 17).

The main point (vv. 14-15) is that Paul discovered that God has a new way of dealing with human beings: with mercy. He presents his insight in terms of "then" and "now"– once a blasphemer, now mercifully treated (see also Gal 1:11-24; Phil 3:3-11). His previous behavior was total perversity since it involved all three symbolic body zones: blaspheme = mouth/ears; persecute = hands/feet; arrogance = heart/eyes. His excuse was ignorance and unbelief, which means failing to perceive or understand that God would develop a new way of serving him apart from the Law.

Appreciating God's new way of accepting human beings was as difficult for the pagans of Ephesus to appreciate as it was for a Judean like Paul. Popular Stoic philosophy taught that a person could find rescue, salvation, and meaning in life through self-sufficiency which would derive from simply living in accord with the laws of nature. The Pastor's statement boldly counters: Jesus brings salvation; it is not self-effected. So startling is this view that the Pastor confirms it: "This saying is trustworthy and deserves full acceptance" (see also 1 Tim 3:1; 4:9; 2 Tim 2:2; Titus 3:3). In a culture where deception and lying are acceptable strategies for defending honor and reputation, this is how one insists one is telling the truth. Even if the statements following this insistence come from liturgy or creeds, they still indicate how challenging it was to accept such notions.

Today's gospel (Luke 15:1-32) recounts how Jesus' practice of welcoming sinners and eating with them piqued the Pharisees and scribes who knew perfectly well how to please God, or so they thought. Jesus and the Pastor offer good critiques in their respective settings. What lesson does the Pastor suggest for the contemporary reader's setting?

Twenty-Fifth Sunday in Ordinary Time
1 Timothy 2:1-8

The conclusion (3:14-16) to the section (1 Tim 2:1–3:13) in which today's verses are located claims to have presented guidelines for honorable behavior in the local church, God's household. Today's verses offer guidelines for prayer. Notice the different words for prayer in this passage: supplications, prayers, petitions, thanksgiving. Literally in Greek, prayers are "approaches to God." Supplications and intercessions ordinarily describe formal petitions to a king at an audience. Thanksgivings are characteristic Israelite prayers. What these have in common are that they are forms of communication, which is what prayer is essentially.

What is the purpose of this prayer? "That we may lead a quiet and tranquil life in all devotion and dignity" (v. 2). The Pastor has frequently been accused of accepting the prevailing ethic of his time and failing to go beyond it. Yet, except where this conduct would openly contradict a teaching of Jesus, it would be almost impossible for the Pastor to do anything else. Believers must be at least as visibly good as their pagan neighbors.

Finally, the repetition of "all" and "everyone" gives this passage a universal tone. Some of the Pastor's contemporaries, the Gnostics, divided humankind into categories: spiritual people who were definitely going to be saved; material people who were not. Further, Gnostics and Israelites believed in a variety of mediators: Moses (Gal 3:19); angels (Heb 2:5-8); the high priest, et al. The Pastor says Jesus is the only mediator between God and ALL humankind, a powerful blow against naysayers.

Finally, the Pastor adds an interesting note about the posture for prayer. Notice the posture involved all three symbolic body zones: pray (mouth/ears), lifted hands (hands/feet), and without anger (heart/eyes) or argument (mouth/ears). All three zones must be properly aligned, or in modern terms, the one who prays ought to have "her/his act together." (Relative to "holy" hands, around A.D. 235 Hippolytus required that a Christian wash hands before praying.)

In today's gospel (Luke 16:1-13), the master commended the clever steward for getting his act together when he sensed the prospect of losing his position, status, and livelihood. Jesus in his parable, the steward in his behavior, and the Pastor in his advice on prayer all demonstrate an awareness of how to communicate well to attain one's heart's desire.

Twenty-Sixth Sunday in Ordinary Time
1 Timothy 6:11-16

Winding up his letter, the Pastor reminds Timothy and all Church leaders to align their teaching with respectful conduct to be manifested in five other-directed virtues. Previously the Pastor referred to Timothy as child or son (1 Tim 1:2, 18), but now he calls him "man of God." This phrase is commonly used in Scripture to describe someone who is in God's service, who speaks on God's behalf, or who holds God's place in the community (Deut 33:1; Josh 14:6; 1 Sam 9:6; etc.). It is one more attempt on the Pastor's part to reactivate and strengthen Timothy's understandably sagging commitment to God and to his ministry. Verses 15-16 are a hymn fragment which praises God as the blessed and sole ruler, the One who stands at the very top of the ladder of worthies to whom is due respectful conduct.

The man who considered himself worthy and "on top of the heap" in today's gospel parable (Luke 16:19-31) winds up with status reversed in alternate reality. The Pastor reminds Church leaders to grasp well that God is in charge, and God's ministers ought to remain faithful in ministering to others. Pity the leader or minister who becomes convinced of an exaggerated sense of self-importance.

Twenty-Seventh Sunday in Ordinary Time
2 Timothy 1:6-8, 13-14

Today's verses, read along with 1 Cor 16:10-11, do not paint a very flattering picture of a Church leader. The Pastor has to urge this fellow to "stir into flame," rekindle or keep alive God's grace (v. 6). He should not be timid ("spirit of cowardice," a lack of courage or moral strength, v. 7). Neither should he be ashamed (v. 8) of witnessing to the Lord or of Paul. This last comment is particularly striking. Honor, the core cultural value here, requires in part that every person recognize and respect those who have power over life at every level. The Pastor has already identified Timothy as "my dear son" (2 Tim 1:2). This is more than an endearing phrase. It carries a hook, and here in v. 8 the Pastor yanks the hook. How dare a "child" dishonor a father by being ashamed of him? Unthinkable, unacceptable, almost unpardonable!

Honor also requires that a person hold proper attitudes and exhibit appropriate behaviors toward others who control existence, namely, God and his son, Jesus. Timothy ought not be ashamed of witnessing to the Lord. So on the basis of very fundamental constituent elements of honor, the Pastor seeks to call Timothy back to honorable behavior. Timothy's timidity, cooled ardor, and feelings of shame are significant shortcomings in an honor-driven culture. In a leader, such failures are devastating. The Pastor offers Church leaders the positive example of Paul which is worth imitating. It was common for teachers to exhort disciples to imitate and share in their striving for perfection. The Pastor concludes with a pointed instruction that this Church leader should guard the deposit of faith, that is, the good things which have been entrusted to him (v. 14) and to take as a norm and model the sound or true words the Pastor has spoken (v. 13).

The word translated as "sound" literally means "healthy" and draws its force from the context of human health and well-being. In antiquity, human health and well-being included much more than physical considerations. All health and well-being problems pertained to the larger meaning of life and life's "rules." Salvation meant restoration of meaning to life. A savior was one who could restore meaning to life. Now consider the Pastor's advice to a discouraged Church leader. Follow my example of steadfastness and fidelity to the gospel, even if it bring suffering in its wake. It was common for teachers to exhort disciples to imitate and share in their striving for perfection. The Pastor reminds Timothy that God has saved us or restored meaning to our lives through Jesus Christ our Savior. You, Timothy, along with other Church leaders, ought to guard this spiritual trust (v. 14). I don't mean memorizing precise sentences (as in 1 Cor 15:1-5), but rather see to it that your message is sound and healthy, that is, life-giving and life-enriching. Anything else is life-denying or impoverishes the true meaning and purpose in life.

The disciples in today's gospel (Luke 17:5-10) ask Jesus to "increase our faith" (= loyalty). The Pastor sought to increase, nay, to restore Timothy's faith (= loyalty). Faith is a gift that requires diligent attention. There is no shame in asking for help when needed, and those like the Pastor who can help others in this regard should do so even without being asked.

Twenty-Eighth Sunday in Ordinary Time
2 Timothy 2:8-13

Continuing his efforts to rejuvenate Timothy, raise his spirit, and restore his confidence, the Pastor repeats Paul's gospel: Jesus is Messiah, descended from David, and raised from the dead. Infatuation with saviors in this cultural world is what brings the evangelist grief when he claims Jesus is THE savior. (The Greek word for savior appears only in Phil 3:20 among the undisputed Pauline letters, but ten times in the Pastorals: 1 Tim 1:1; 2:3; 4:10; 2 Tim 1:10; Titus 1:3, 4; 2:10, 13; 3:4, 6.) Jesus robbed death of its power and brought life and immortality to us because he himself was raised from the dead. To champion and promote faith in a savior like this is almost absurd. Not only is the very idea resisted, but the one who promotes it is often punished. But Paul bears with suffering for the benefit of the chosen, in the true fashion of a collectivistic personality.

Perhaps because he felt this exhortation needed still more force, the Pastor clusters passages drawn from an already existing tradition and guarantees that they are trustworthy, namely, that he speaks truth and is not being deceptive. These sayings derived from community experience, reflection, and discernment. They were accepted as trustworthy, reliable pieces of advice for newcomers as well as worthwhile reminders and handy norms for veteran believers.

The first two are comforting. "If we have died with him, we shall also live with him" (compare 1 Cor 15:31; 2 Cor 4:8-11; Rom 6:8). The community has grown accustomed to repeating this sentiment. It makes sense out of life by nourishing hope. "If we persevere we shall also reign with him" (compare 2 Cor 1:5, 7; Rom 8:17). The descending order of human response in both statements (die, continue to persevere) still gains a reward (life, rule).

The third statement continues this descending order of human response to suffering, but gives the modern reader slight pause. "If we deny him he will deny us." Childish tit-for-tat? No, quite in accord with the Jesus tradition (Matt 10:33; Mark 8:38; Luke 12:8-10). To deny Jesus is to act shamefully, so this statement is actually an attempt to motivate the believer to avoid shame by behaving honorably.

The final verse brings this cluster of aphorisms to a conclusion in paradox (compare Rom 3:3-8; 11:29-32). This is the heart of Paul's gospel of grace. What God shares with us in Jesus is pure gift. Not even suffering can win God's favor! Moreover, Jesus' response to infidelity is unwavering fidelity and unbounded love. How do you think Jesus might have reacted to the other nine sick people in today's gospel (Luke 17:11-19) the next time he met them, as was quite likely to happen? To say "thank you" in this culture ends a relationship. The nine Judeans wouldn't dream of ending a relationship with a fellow Judean, Jesus, whose help they might need in the future. Nevertheless, as the Pastor observes: "If we are unfaithful he [God] remains faithful." Good news in every age.

Twenty-Ninth Sunday in Ordinary Time
2 Timothy 3:14–4:2

Once again, the Pastor presents the personal example of Paul as he suggests the contrasting posture Timothy ought to propose relative to false teachers. Moreover, in these verses the Pastor explains why Timothy ought to be unswerving in what he has learned and believed. Although his opponents (evil men, imposters, charlatans) might seem to be making headway, they are actually moving in reverse: from bad to worse! In contrast, Timothy learned the faith from reliable and trustworthy transmitters of tradition, like his mother and grandmother who in that culture have nearly exclusive contact with boys until the age of puberty (2 Tim 1:4), from Paul (2 Tim 3:10), and from the Scriptures themselves (2 Tim 3:15). The word "scripture" very likely refers to the Hebrew Scriptures, the Old Testament. It was Irenaeus in A.D. 180 who first used the word "New Testament" as a reference to Christian writings. Still, they were known, revered, and quoted (see 1 Tim 5:18 which cites Deut 25:4 and Luke 10:7).

As all readers probably know, 2 Tim 3:15 is the classic text that speaks of the inspiration of Scripture. This passage needs to be understood and interpreted with its literary and cultural context. The literary context of this letter is certainly "false teachers." Beginning in 2 Tim 2:14, with the focus on deception, lying, false teaching, susceptibility of many to these false teachers, it is difficult to miss the Pastor's concern. From a cultural perspective, when one remembers that secrecy, deception, and lying are commonplace and acceptable strategies in the service of honor, it is easy to become hopelessly discouraged and throw up one's hands in despair. It is in this context that the Pastor reminds Timothy and Church leaders to trust their sources: mothers/ grandmothers (the first teachers), Paul, and the Scripture "breathed" by God who doesn't lie. (See 1 Kgs 22:23. Ahab is a faithless member of God's family—lying to such a one as this is understandable and culturally acceptable.)

Thus the Pastor reassures the wavering Church leader, Timothy, that what he learned from Scripture would literally instruct him in salvation, that is, the true meaning, purpose, and goal of life as manifest now in the quality and direction of the life of Messiah Jesus. Therefore, he must proclaim the word whether convenient or inconvenient. In today's gospel (Luke 18:1-8), Jesus urges his disciples to pray without becoming weary. This is the same advice the Pastor offers to Timothy and through him to Church leaders about preaching. Whether praying or preaching, remaining steadfast is essential, whatever it takes.

Thirtieth Sunday in Ordinary Time
2 Timothy 4:6-8, 16-18

These final, personal remarks create a clear impression that Paul feels deserted and abandoned (vv. 6-8). He sounds as if he is on the verge of death. The images are drawn from Paul's own letters: libation (Phil 2:17), race (1 Cor 9:24; Phil 3:12), crown (1 Cor 9:25). Yet if he is truly on the verge of death, his request for a visit from Timothy would entail a journey of three or four months; perhaps death was not that imminent. The Pastor realizes that though he has repeatedly urged the recipients of this letter not to be ashamed, the fact is that fidelity to the truth of the gospel may cost them friendships. They will feel and may actually be deserted and abandoned. Perhaps they may also wish for death. Not to fret! Paul had no less trying experiences.

Despite his situation, Paul manages to maintain a high level of confidence (vv. 15-18). Though no one spoke up at a preliminary legal hearing, Paul is forgiving after the pattern presented by Luke 23:34 and Acts 7:60. The Lord gave him strength, and the Lord will continue to rescue him—and anyone else who needs rescue!

Throughout these verses, Paul is displayed as a living embodiment of all he is purported to have written here—a flesh and blood model worthy of emulation. The high esteem in which communities held Paul after his death would make him a compelling motivating force for perseverance in the good news. Certainly, the tax collector in today's gospel parable (Luke 18:9-14) could have used an encouraging word. Like the Pastor, all believers should stay aware of people and situations that could benefit from an uplifting thought and a pledge of solidarity.

Thirty-First Sunday in Ordinary Time
2 Thessalonians 1:11–2:2

Writing in the name of Paul perhaps around the year A.D. 80 or 90, the pseudonymous author of this letter sounds a strong warning against a deceptive opinion circulating in the community that the Day of the Lord is at hand. It is important to remember that secrecy, deception, and lying are acceptable and normal strategies for protecting one's reputation in the honor-driven Middle Eastern world. It was extremely difficult to know whether or not a person was telling the truth. To assure the listener of the truth of a statement, the speaker would make an oath (Amen; Amen, I say unto you; or As the Lord lives!).

Today's reading begins with a prayer that God will support the Thessalonians in their faith and thus bring honor to the deity and to them. Only God can bring about this assured result. Prayer is always a form of communication to obtain a result from the one addressed. Here the author hopes to persuade God to remain loyal to those called and designated for divine benevolence.

Having given this word of assurance, the author now pleads that the Thessalonians stand firm in their faith and not allow themselves to be deceived at the coming Day of the Lord. Rumors persisted that the event was imminent. Some of the rumors were alleged to have originated with a "spirit," a

supra-human agent closer to God than humans and therefore more informed and reliable. The rumor may have been
circulating in a variety of forms: an oral report, a sermon, a
forged letter—we can't be certain. In a cultural world perme-
ated by deception, it would be nearly impossible to confirm
or disprove the rumor. Hence the clever strategy of this
pseudonymous author to trade on the authority of Paul in
order to keep calm in the community. The core of the author's message is that the Day of the Lord is less a calendri-
cal date than an event: the gathering of all believers to meet
the Lord and thus to obtain the fulfillment of faith-life.

In today's gospel (Luke 19:1-10), Zacchaeus sought Jesus
who in turn came to Zacchaeus' house and publicly declared
that the opinions of the townsfolk were mistaken: Zacchaeus
was not a "sinner man" as they thought, but a true descendant of Abraham. The author of Second Thessalonians seeks
to assure the Thessalonians that the rumors about the Day
of the Lord are erroneous. They should not believe them.
Isn't it comforting to know there will always be someone in
the community to help separate gossip from sure knowledge
in matters of faith?

Thirty-Second Sunday in Ordinary Time
2 Thessalonians 2:16–3:5

Verses 16 and 17 are yet another prayer in this letter unusual for such frequent mention of prayer. Once again, the author prays that God encourage and strengthen the Thessalonians deeply troubled and disturbed by vicious and erroneous rumors about the Day of the Lord. The sure basis for such encouragement is that God has attached himself to the chosen. Love, in the biblical world, is group-glue, cohesion, that which holds people or a community together. Since we know God has done this, we can be confident God won't become "unglued" from us.

A second gift of God is identified as "good hope." This phrase was common in the Mystery Religions in antiquity (e.g., those of Cybele, Mithras, or Orpheus) that helped human beings negotiate high points in life from birth to death: marriage, choice of career, meetings with outstanding persons, etc. Devotees of the Mystery Religions understood "good hope" to describe bliss after death. One should not fear the end of life but look forward to what comes next. This author writing in the name of Paul modifies the concept by linking it with "everlasting encouragement"—something they urgently needed in the present moment—and also linking it with "through his grace." Christian "good hope" rests on the Lord's victorious return.

In the concluding prayer (2 Thess 3:1-5), the author asks the Thessalonians to pray for him, too. Keep in mind that prayer is essentially a mode of communication whereby the speaker hopes to move or motivate the listener. Having prayed for the letter recipients throughout the letter, the author now hopes they will reciprocate. In that cultural world, evil was mixed in with the good. Perverse and wicked people of no faith work against evangelizers like the author of this letter. The bedrock of confidence, however, is the Lord who remains loyal. The Lord will protect against evil people and will see to it that the Thessalonians will indeed put into practice the preaching they have heard. What counts above all is love of (adherence to) God and the stick-to-it-iveness of Jesus.

Today's gospel (Luke 20:27-38) features the Sadducees who deny the resurrection. The episode presents a nice foil to the epistle which "Christianizes" the pagan idea of "good hope" and roots it in the victorious return of the Lord when all believers will be gathered to him. Both readings invite modern believers to reflect on resurrection and its meaning in the contemporary Christian world.

Thirty-Third Sunday in Ordinary Time
2 Thessalonians 3:7-12

The key word here is "disorderly" (vv. 7 and 11, sometimes inappropriately translated "idle"). One of Paul's obsessions very evident in his authentic letters is order in the communities. A place for everything and everyone, and everyone and everything in its place. Disorder is a major threat to communal well-being. Thus the pseudonymous author of this letter once again manages to adduce a Pauline virtue by trading on his name. It allows him to present himself as a role model: "We wanted to present ourselves as a model for you, so that you might imitate us" (v. 9).

The example given by Paul is voluntarily foregoing his right to a remuneration for preaching. In the ancient Middle East, where economics as we know and love it in the West did not yet exist, people interacted by means of an implied dyadic contract. I do you a favor, now you owe me. You repay my favor, I owe you again. On the basis of this cultural principle, Jesus could send his apostles out to preach and urge them not to be weighed down with excess baggage which would impede the mission (Luke 9:1-6). If the locals did not support the preachers, they were to move on.

While the dyadic contract is a legitimate cultural strategy by which peasants could make a go of it in difficult circumstances, it could also be abused. A person might delay or "forget" to repay the favor but expect still other favors. Such a person would have time to "mind the business of others" and stir up problems, foment division in the community. The advice is to mind one's own business and take care of oneself until they learn mutual reciprocity.

"Minding the business of others" is actually a common pastime in the Mediterranean world of antiquity and the present. The Greek word here is "busy-body." Privacy is relatively unknown in that world. In group-oriented or collectivistic cultures (representing 80 percent of the planet's population at the present time), people control others by watching over them, threatening to shame them with gossip if they misbehave, ruining their reputations, and publicly dishonoring them. In the West, we are guided by an internalized set of principles we usually call conscience. But in the Middle East, conscience is public scrutiny of behavior. It is quite external. The author of this letter recognizes its devastating consequences and urges, "in the Lord Jesus Christ," that they refrain from such behavior. His advice very likely was not heeded.

In the gospel (Luke 21:5-19), Jesus cautions his followers that people will gossip and lie about them, but they are not to prepare a defense. He will give "a wisdom in speaking." It is difficult to remember such a promise in trying circumstances, but hearing the promise repeated should give modern believers a better perspective on the trials of life so often provided by fellow human beings and even believers.

Thirty-Fourth Sunday in Ordinary Time (Christ the King)
Colossians 1:12-20

[For background, see Fifteenth Sunday in Ordinary Time.] Beginning in v. 15, the sacred author introduces a primitive Christian hymn originating perhaps in the liturgy. Differences in the vocabulary, style, and thought content from the rest of Colossians and from the undisputed Paulines confirms this judgment. It is similar to hymns found in Qumran and to the prologue of John's Gospel (1:1-18). The theme of the hymn is the role of Jesus in creation.

The Hellenistic Judaic tradition claimed that wisdom, which was created first, was also an agent or partner in YHWH's work of creation. Wisdom motifs are echoed throughout this hymn (Wis 7:22; 9:2-4; see also Prov 3:19; 8:22-31). A key idea, however, is that Jesus is the "image" of the invisible God (v. 15). Medieval Franciscan theologians like John Duns Scotus used this hymn to argue the absolute primacy of Christ. In order for the invisible God to create a human being in the divine image and likeness, God needed a model. Jesus incarnate, "the firstborn of all creation," was the model and image. The philosophical axiom that the first thing one thinks of (e.g., a cake) is the last thing to happen (after gathering ingredients, mixing, then baking) fleshed out the argument. God thought of Jesus incarnate first and eventually, in the course of time (which doesn't affect God), Jesus was born.

In Jesus all other created beings in the sky and on earth, visible and invisible, whether angelic or astral, came into being. He is indeed the head of the cosmic body, but the sacred author appears to have added "the church" in v. 18, shifting the image to Jesus as head of the Church which is an important theme in Col (1:24, 27; 2:17, 19; 3:15). The community as body is certainly present in the authentic Paulines, but Christ as head of the body is a later development.

As the hymn concludes, it praises Jesus as preeminent and reconciling all things, thus establishing and solidifying unity in the entire cosmos and in the Church. The gospel (Luke 22:35-43) reports the tradition at Jesus' trial in which a claim to the title of "king" for him was questioned. Still, his promise to the criminal that "today you will be with me in Paradise" suggests something of Jesus' power given by God, as today's hymn from Colossians indicates, from all time at the very beginning of creation. While this feast has medieval theological roots and was instituted for the universal Church in 1925 by Pope Pius XI, our ancestors in the faith whose thinking is reflected in Colossians actually laid a solid foundation. On this occasion, modern worshipers have an opportunity to consider the importance of historical knowledge in appreciating their faith heritage.

Recommended Resources

Elliott, John H. "Paul, Galatians, and the Evil Eye." *Currents in Theology and Mission* 17 (1990) 262–73.

Malina, Bruce J., and John J. Pilch. *Social Science Commentary on the Book of Revelation.* Minneapolis: Fortress Press, 2000.

Malina, Bruce J., and Jerome H. Neyrey. *Portraits of Paul: An Archaeology of Ancient Personality.* Louisville, Ky.: Westminster John Knox Press, 1996.

Murphy-O'Connor, Jerome. *Paul: A Critical Life.* New York and Oxford: Oxford University Press, 1997.

_____. *Paul the Letter-Writer: His World, His Options, His Skills.* Collegeville: The Liturgical Press, 1995.

Neyrey, Jerome H. *Paul in Other Words: A Cultural Reading of His Letters.* Louisville, Ky.: Westminster John Knox Press, 1994.

Pilch, John J. *The Cultural Dictionary of the Bible.* Collegeville: The Liturgical Press, 1999.

_____. *The Cultural World of Jesus Sunday by Sunday: Cycle C.* Collegeville: The Liturgical Press, 1997.

_____. *Galatians and Romans.* The Collegeville Bible Commentary 6. Collegeville: The Liturgical Press, 1982.

_____. "Illuminating the World of Jesus through Cultural Anthropology." *The Living Light* 31 (1994) 20–31. http://www.georgetown. edu/faculty/pilchj/ click on: "Mediterranean Culture."

_____. *The Triduum: Breaking Open the Scriptures.* Collegeville: The Liturgical Press, 2000.

Sloyan, Gerard S. "What Kind of Canon Do the Lectionaries Constitute?" *Biblical Theology Bulletin* 30 (2000) 27–35.

Websites

Roman Catholic Lectionary for Mass:
http://clawww.lmu.edu/faculty/fjust/Lectionary.htm

Revised Common Lectionary:
http://divinity.library.vanderbilt.edu/lectionary